THE MARSHALL CAVENDISH
☆ ☆ ☆ ILLUSTRATED ☆ ☆ ☆
ENCYCLOPEDIA OF
WORLD WAR II

VOLUME 7

THE MARSHALL CAVENDISH
☆ ☆ ☆ ILLUSTRATED ☆ ☆ ☆
ENCYCLOPEDIA OF

WORLD WAR II

Based on the original text by
Lieutenant Colonel Eddy Bauer

CONSULTANT EDITOR

Brigadier General James L. Collins, Jr., U.S.A.

CHIEF OF MILITARY HISTORY,
DEPARTMENT OF THE ARMY

MARSHALL CAVENDISH CORPORATION/NEW YORK

CONTENTS

Editorial Director: Brian Innes
Editor-in-chief; Brigadier Peter Young, D.S.O., M.C., M.A.
Managing Editor: Richard Humble
Editor: Christopher Chant
Art Editor: Jim Bridge

THE TIDE TURNS

CHAPTER 62

Crisis in the Desert

△ *Churchill, whose dispute with Auchinleck about the progress of operations in the North African theatre was eventually to cost the latter his command.*
▷ *A German crew in action with a piece of heavy artillery. Such artillery, together with minefields, formed the backbone of the major defensive positions from which Rommel launched his armoured outflanking movements.*

If the insolent passage through the Straits of Dover by Vice-Admiral Ciliax's squadron provoked such an outburst of discontent in Britain, it was also because, coming only three days before the fall of Singapore, it had followed on the defeat, as unexpected as it was remarkable, of the 8th Army in North Africa. This latter had brought the Axis forces from the El Agheila–Marada line to a line Gazala–Bir Hakeim. And what would British opinion have made of it all if it had also been informed of the enormous successes of Admiral Dönitz between Cape Sable in Nova Scotia and the Mississippi delta?

Under the influence of the pessimism caused by this succession of bad news, some put it about in the corridors of the House of Commons that it was time that Winston Churchill's duties were reduced merely to those of Prime Minister and that the Ministry of Defence should be entrusted to another person, such as Anthony Eden. In his memoirs Churchill makes no mention of this intrigue and, as can well be imagined, those responsible for it took good care not to boast about it.

Churchill had his own very personal way of illustrating his theories, as is shown by this story he told about the effect of surprise, which could all too often be decisive during the course of a battle:

"I have often tried to set down the strategic truths I have comprehended in the form of simple anecdotes. One of them is the celebrated tale of the man who gave the powder to the bear. He mixed the powder with the greatest care, making sure that not only the ingredients but the proportions were absolutely correct. He rolled it up in a large paper spill and was about to blow it down the bear's throat. But the bear blew first."

These intrigues against the Prime Minister are, however, revealed to us in Sir Arthur Bryant's "presentation" of Lord Alanbrooke's war note-books. Sir Arthur's reputation as a scrupulous and independent historian is well known.

To the great good fortune of Britain and the Commonwealth, and therefore to the nations who were their allies, this scheme was nipped in the bud; had it succeeded it would probably have caused a series of political crises. In fact, one can hardly imagine the Prime Minister confining himself to the figurehead rôle envisaged for him, convinced as he was that he incarnated that sense of strategy which had amounted to genius in his ancestor John Churchill, Duke of Marlborough. He could not have failed to interest himself in the conduct of operations, and his Minister of Defence would never have tolerated the daily intrusion of the Prime Minister in his sphere of responsibilities. Further conflicts would have been inevitable.

On the other hand, when the two great warring coalitions were balanced on the knife-edge of destiny, Britain and the United Nations would have been without the drive of the man whose part in the Allies' final victories Sir Arthur Bryant has defined by saying:

"When it came to the political direction of war–to seeing and expressing its broad, fundamental truths in terms that men and nations could understand and translate into action–the Prime Minister had no equal."

Trouble in North Africa

However that might be, at the beginning of this year of 1942, British strategy in the Middle East most disastrously reflected the increasing menace of events in the Far East.

We have seen how, when it reached the Cape, the 18th Division, originally intended for General Auchinleck, was redirected to Singapore, where it arrived just in time to be swallowed up in the capitulation of February 15. The 5th Division was also diverted from the Eastern Mediterranean theatre and split up into brigades, some to be used against Diego-Suarez (Operation "Ironclad") and others in Burma.

In addition to these failed expectations, G.H.Q. Cairo also had taken away from it, on orders from London, 150 tanks and three divisions: the 70th, which had defended Tobruk and was sent to Ceylon, and the 6th and 7th Australian which, as we have seen, were sent home at the

◁ ◁ *A motorcycle combination, spearhead of the 21st Panzer Division.*
◁ *German troops help load their vehicles aboard a troopship before embarking to join Rommel in North Africa.*
▽ *A Pzkw III arrives in North Africa. With the arrival of a batch of Pzkw III and IV tanks on January 5, Major Mellenthin, Rommel's chief Intelligence officer, was able to report that the Axis would have armoured superiority in front of El Agheila.*

urgent request of Prime Minister Curtin.

Far from receiving the reinforcements he thought he could count on, Air Chief-Marshal Tedder, Air Officer Commanding Middle East, had to lose four fighter squadrons. Finally, in face of the Japanese threat to the Indian Ocean, the Admiralty was quite unable to repair the terrible damage caused to the Mediterranean Fleet. Sir Andrew Cunningham had therefore to do as best he could without battleships, aircraft-carriers, and heavy cruisers.

As far as concerns the forces which Sir Arthur Tedder deployed with such skill, their failed expectations arose not only from the fact that new theatres of operations in the Far East were being equipped with formations due to them on the eve of Pearl Harbor, but also because hundreds of fighters and light bombers for the R.A.F. were sent to Murmansk and Archangel, and U.S. military aid to Russia meant that the delivery of planes to Great Britain had had to be slowed down.

But if, for all that and in accordance with the decisions taken at the "Arcadia" Conference, Auchinleck was still requir-

Axis heavy artillery on the move over the flowers of a Cyrenaican spring.

ed to mount Operation "Acrobat", which was to take the 8th Army from Agedabia to the Tunisian frontier, as C.-in-C. British Forces in the Middle East he had other, and too many, fish to fry.

The Prime Minister did not seem to realise this in London and, faced with Auchinleck's reluctance to start his offensive again without delay, he wrote to him on March 15.

"A very heavy German counter-stroke upon the Russians must be expected soon, and it will be thought intolerable that the 635,000 men (exclusive of Malta) on your ration strength should remain unengaged, preparing for another set-piece battle in July."

British divisions too scattered

In effect, when this message was being sent, G.H.Q. Cairo had under its command 16 divisions from Britain and the Dominions. But this did not mean that it could use them as it wished. On the contrary, nine of them were on politico-military duties which had nothing to do with the conduct of operations in the North African theatre of war, and they could not be taken off these without the prior consent of the War Cabinet.

Two of them were keeping order in Abyssinia. Three others, one in Cyprus and two in Syria, were bolstering up the morale of Turkey, which might fall at any moment into the opposite camp under threat of an invasion thought to be imminent from the Dodecanese. Finally, occupying Iraq and Persia were four divisions, three of them Indian, ready to stop any advance by the Germans were they to occupy the Caucasus and move on the Persian Gulf to mop up the Middle East oilfields. Thus the enemy was to be met wherever he might appear. It must be said, however, that given the time it would take the Panzers to get from the Khar'kov area to Batumi and Baku, the British forces could have been concentrated and crushed Rommel. When he set sail from Cadiz on October 21, 1805, the unhappy Admiral Villeneuve signalled to his captains: "Every man who is not under fire is not at his post." The fact that he was defeated several hours later does not detract from the force of this essential principle.

△ *Allied armour's main enemy: a German gunner with an 8.8-cm round.*
▷ *Brothers-in-arms who could not see eye to eye: Rommel (right) with his nominal superior, the Italian Marshal Ettore Bastico, commander of the Axis forces in North Africa.*

Mediterranean Sea

Apollonia
Beda Littoria
Luigi Razza
Cirene
Derna
El Garib
El Fadja
Tokra
Maraua
Bersis
Barce
Slonta
Bomba
Tecnis
3.2.42
Driana
27.1.42
El Abiar
Tmimi
Benghazi
Er Regima
Mechili
Barca
4th Indian Div.

Ghemines
Soluch
Msus
Tengeder

Gulf of Sirte
Antelat
Saunnu

German
S. Frag
Italian
Agedabia
British

Marsa Brega
El Agheila
Ghemines
Soluch
Msus
0   25 miles
21.1.42
7th Armd. Div.
Beda Fomm
Antelat
21st Pz. Div.
15th Pz. Div.
"Ariete" Div.
Saunnu
Gruppe Marcks
Agedabia
"Trieste" Mot. Div.
Giof Megraf
"Sabratha" Div.
El Grara
El Fenscia
1st Armd. Div.

Marada
0   50 miles

◁ Rommel's swift drive to the Gulf of Bomba. The British, caught in the midst of a re-deployment, nevertheless managed to extricate most of their forces from the trap prepared by Rommel.
▽ Rommel. His lightning spring offensive was as great a surprise to the Italian and German staffs as to the British.
◁▽ German heavy artillery just before the beginning of the offensive.

Rommel's surprise attack

The last days of 1941 had seen a complete reversal of the situation in the Central Mediterranean: the destruction of Force K, based on Malta, the battering of the island-fortress by the concentrated efforts of the Italian Air Force and II and X *Fliegerkorps* of the Luftwaffe, the weakening of the Mediterranean Fleet—all this had reopened the route to Tripoli to the Axis convoys. Whereas in December, taking into account losses of 19 per cent, only 39,902 tons of war *matériel* and fuel had been landed, in January 100 per cent of all replacements and supplies loaded in Italy got through to Africa. These amounted to 43,328 tons of *matériel* and 22,842 tons of liquid fuel. On January 5 one convoy brought in for the *Afrika Korps* 54 Pzkw III and IV tanks, 20 armoured cars, and some self-propelled guns, Russian 76.2-mm guns on Czech tank chassis, all complete with their crews. For its part, the Italian Mobile Corps, now under the command of General Zingales, got two groups of *semoventi*, Italian-made 75-mm self-propelled guns which proved very effective. Altogether the Axis armoured strength taken by Rommel out of the El Agheila–Marada line, which was henceforth held by only the Italian XXI and

X Corps, was 84 German medium and heavy tanks and 89 Italian medium tanks on January 11, 1942. A further 28 German tanks, newly arrived at Tripoli, were expected to join him soon.

Rommel therefore decided to counterattack, taking advantage immediately of

△ △ *A British Crusader tank at speed during the retreat to Benghazi.*
△ *Lieutenant-General N. M. Ritchie, commander of the 8th Army* (right) *with Lieutenant-General C. W. M. Norrie, commander of XXX Corps.*

his enemy's scattered forces and hoping thus to catch him by surprise, thin on the ground. He issued the following order of the day to his troops:

"German and Italian soldiers:

"You have already endured hard battles against an enemy vastly superior in numbers to yourselves. Your fighting spirit has not been daunted. We now have material superiority over the enemy in front of us. The army will go over to the attack today to wipe him out.

"I expect every man to give of his best in these decisive days. Long live Italy! Long live Greater Germany! Long live their leaders!"

Surprise was complete, not only at the front for the British XIII Corps and at Cairo for Sir Claude Auchinleck, but at Homs, where he happened to be at the time, for General Bastico and at Rome, both for the *Comando Supremo* and for Field-Marshal Kesselring. In the entry in his diary for January 21 Rommel explains his silence in terms which give cause for reflection:

"I had maintained secrecy over the Panzer Group's forthcoming attack eastwards from Marsa Brega and informed neither the Italian nor the German High Command. We knew from experience that Italian Headquarters cannot keep things to themselves and that everything they wireless to Rome gets round to British ears. However, I had arranged with the Quartermaster for the Panzergruppe's order to be posted up in every Cantoniera (Road Maintenance Depot) in Tripolitania on the 21st January – the day the attack was due to take place."

Without expressing an opinion of the danger of the leaks in Rome which he feared, and which in his view entitled him to deploy the Italian troops under him without reference to General Bastico, we would observe that he did not need to fear such leaks at O.K.W. If Rommel kept his intentions secret from his superiors it was because he feared they would forbid him from carrying them out.

The Benghazi road cut

In the first part of this battle Rommel found himself facing the British 1st Armoured Division. Newly arrived in Africa, it had only 150 tanks, and had been split into three groups which could not be self-supporting. The same dispersion was evident at the next level upwards, XIII Corps: the 4th Indian Division which, for logistic reasons, had got no further forward than Benghazi, could not help the 1st Armoured, and the latter was even less likely to get help from the 7th Armoured Division, which had

▽ *Benghazi, the first objective of Rommel's offensive, which fell on January 28.*

△ An Axis petrol dump. Such was the toll taken by British planes and submarines operating from Malta that fuel for the Axis vehicles became the single most limiting factor in Rommel's plans.

▷ Preparing the vital aerial umbrella: armourers harmonise the guns of a Messerschmitt 109 fighter. Although the British had overall superiority in the air, the Germans were able to obtain local predominance over major offensives at the expense of denuding their rear areas of fighter cover.

been sent back to Tobruk to be brought up to strength.

Moving forward along two axes of attack with five armoured and motorised divisions, the Italian Mobile Corps along the Via Balbia and the *Afrika Korps* further inland, Rommel had no difficulty in sweeping before him the 22nd Guards Brigade and, in the evening of January 22, he camped at Agedabia, having advanced 56 miles in 48 hours. In particular he had cut the road to Benghazi, to the surprise and dismay of his enemy. The following day he set about the destruction of the opposing forces by an encircling movement. Whilst General Zingales engaged the bulk of the 1st Armoured Division in the west, he drove the *Afrika Korps* northeast towards Antelat then turned southeast, and due south from Saunnu. However, in its haste to close the trap round the enemy, his vanguard left Saunnu before the head of the 15th Panzer Division reached it and the British escaped through the gap, though in a bad state and leaving a great deal of *matériel* behind.

Rommel again held back by the Italians

Meanwhile, alerted by Bastico, Marshal Cavallero, sent by plane to the battle-front by Mussolini, appeared in Rommel's headquarters to tighten the reins on this bold *Panzerwaffe* charger. In a directive dated January 23 he drew Rommel's attention to the general situation:

"The conduct of the war in Tripolitania is a function of the situation in the Mediterranean. It is possible that, owing to a shortage of diesel oil, our convoys might be reduced or even stop altogether from mid-February. It must be expected, however, that the effects of our intensive action on Malta will help considerably the despatch, already under way, of isolated ships by the western route, but this will scarcely be enough to ensure the normal feeding of our colony and no more troops or *matériel* can be expected."

Taking into account possible enemy action, including an "Anglo-Gaullist" landing in Tunisia or on the Libyan coast, or even of an attack from the Sahara, Cavallero, acting in the name of the Duce, drew up the following instructions based on the above premises:

1. In the east the line of resistance was still Marsa Brega–Marada, which the major infantry units were not to pass.
2. As for the mobile forces, intended to disorganise the enemy's preparations for attack, they would carry out "limited range operations" whenever the opportunity arose.

If he had obeyed these instructions, Rommel would have had to send his mobile forces back over the Marsa Brega–Marada line. He did nothing of the kind, arguing that the situation had overtaken the orders and, making a show of driving towards Mechili, where, remembering his first offensive, General Ritchie was waiting for him, he appeared unexpectedly outside Benghazi in the evening of January 27. He almost took the 4th Indian Division with him, but it managed to break free, albeit at the cost of over 4,000 killed, wounded, and missing. On February 3, the forward units of the *Afrika Korps*, after bypassing Derna, reached the Gulf of Bomba and on that day the victor captured 3,300 prisoners, 377 armoured vehicles, 192 guns, and 1,200 vehicles.

From all evidence, General Ritchie, C.-in-C. 8th Army, had been caught unprepared, then overtaken by events, and the orders and counter-orders which had been showered on Lieutenant-General Godwin-Austen caused him to ask to be relieved of his command. Major-General Frank Messervy had just taken over command of the British 1st Armoured Division from his wounded colleague Lumsden; he cannot therefore be held responsible for the misadventures which Rommel inflicted on the division.

Promotion for Rommel

On the Axis side, the "limited range offensive operation" envisaged in the January 23 directive had taken Rommel more than 375 miles from his base. This act of insubordination had certainly been crowned with success, but its author was only going to be more inclined to ignore the advice, even when better motivated, of *Comando Supremo*. This was all the more likely because the Führer had promoted his *Panzergruppe* to the grade of *Panzerarmee* (though without giving him any more men or *matériel*) and had promoted him Colonel-General, thus giving him virtual equality with his Italian colleagues.

△ Simplicissimus *of Munich mocks the 8th Army's latest setbacks in Libya: "It's a long, long way to Tripoli-i . . ."*

"ROMMEL, ROMMEL, ROMMEL! Whatever matters but beating him?"

(CHURCHILL)

Born on November 15, 1891 in Heidenheim, a small town in Württemberg, near Ulm, Rommel was the son of a schoolmaster.

Nothing in his background pointed to a military career, but in 1910 he joined the 124th Infantry Regiment as an officer cadet.

In World War I, he "stood out as the perfect fighting animal, cold, cunning, ruthless, untiring, quick of decision, incredibly brave." After seeing action on the Western Front he was promoted to Lieutenant and transferred to a newly formed mountain battalion, the *Württembergische Gebirgsbataillon*; it was with this unit that he reached the climax of his career in World War I. Infiltrating Italian positions southwest of Caporetto, he captured Monte Matajur on October 26, 1917, and with it 150 officers, 9,000 men and 81 guns. He had led his *Abteilung* (detachment) for 50 hours non-stop, covered 12 miles in tough mountainous country, and climbed up to 7,000 feet. He was awarded the Pour le Mérite, and promoted to Captain. Not long after this he was sent on leave and given a staff appointment which he held to the end of the war.

As an officer of recognised ability (the Pour le Mérite was rarely awarded to officers as lowly as lieutenant), he was retained in the *Reichswehr* after the end of World War I. In 1929 he was posted as an instructor to the Infantry School at Dresden where his lectures were published as a book *Infanterie Greift An* (Infantry Attacks). The book covered his personal experiences in Belgium, the Argonne, the Vosges, the Carpathians, and Italy. It became a textbook with the Swiss Army, and caught the attention of Hitler.

When Hitler became Chancellor in 1933, Rommel had had very little contact with German politics. When he was given a special assignment to improve the discipline of the *Hitler Jugend*, he soon clashed with their leader Baldur von Schirach. Rommel felt that the organisation put too much emphasis on sport and military training. The attachment was soon ended and Rommel was able to complete his tour of duty at the War Academy at Potsdam.

In the opening months of Germany's confrontation with the West, Rommel was given the command of Hitler's bodyguard, the *Führerbegleitbataillon*. At Hitler's headquarters he saw that the "new" methods of war were only an adaptation of the tactics used by Ludendorff in 1918, and his own *Abteilung* in Italy and Rumania. Bypass resistance, push into the "soft" areas behind the

1. Field-Marshal Erwin Rommel, Germany's soldier in the sun. The Nazi propaganda industry made him into a cult figure at home, but he was popular with his men in North Africa. Major-General von Mellenthin says "The men knew that Rommel was the last man that Rommel spared; they saw him in their midst and they felt, 'this is our leader'".
2. Rommel in Poland as part of the Führerbegleitbataillon. *His book on infantry tactics and record as a regimental officer in World War I gave him a high reputation even before World War II, but he chafed at an inactive rôle on Hitler's staff at the beginning of the war. Given command of the 7th Panzer Division he handled it with drive and initiative in the invasion of France, breaching the Meuse defences at Houx independently of the main thrust at Sedan.*

2

3

4

5

enemy lines, and spread confusion by appearing unexpectedly: these tactics were now given an edge and range with armoured vehicles, trucks and aircraft, and Rommel wanted to try them.

He got his opportunity in France in 1940.

As commander of the 7th Panzer Division he took his men from the Belgian border to Cherbourg in forty days. At the French naval base he received the surrender of Admiral d'Abrial, four other French admirals, and 30,000 prisoners-of-war.

The 7th Panzer Division, or "Ghost Division" as it came to be nicknamed, was part of Hoth's Panzer group which was in turn part of Rundstedt's Army Group "A".

Advancing from his start-line in Belgium on May 10, Rommel reached the Meuse on the 12th. It was here that he first demonstrated to his division and to his superiors that he was not only courageous, but could handle an armoured division superbly. As his men would discover in Africa, Rommel was an officer who was more at home in the front line than in an office.

It was at Arras that Rommel met his future enemy in Africa. Tanks of the 1st Armoured Division broke through his anti-tank battalion and were only stopped by his 8.8-cm Flak guns. The fighting on May 21 was more costly than any of the earlier actions. In his tank operations he destroyed 43 tanks, but for the loss of 250 men he captured only 50.

Rommel reached Africa on February 12, 1941 and left it for good on March 9, 1943. In the intervening months he fought and out-manoeuvred some of Britain's most experienced soldiers, and earned their respect and the nickname "The Desert Fox". In a conference in Cairo in 1942 Churchill growled "Rommel, Rommel, Rommel! What else matters but beating him?"

The war in North Africa was not like the drive from the borders of Germany in 1940, where fuel and supplies were available "down the road". Tanks were often immobilised for lack of fuel or ammunition, and the *Afrika Korps* soon came to rely on captured vehicles and supplies.

In the thrust and parry of the desert war, there are several victories which are outstanding. The counter-attack and savage fighting after the British "Crusader" offensive of November 1941, and the Gazala battles of May and June 1942 which culminated in the attack on Tobruk on June 20. This time Rommel broke through the defences and captured 25,000 prisoners and General Klopper of the 2nd South African Division. His energy and these victories took the Axis forces past Marsa Matrûh, to Alamein and the gates of Alexandria. But this was his high point, and his attack at Alam Halfa marks the end of the resilience of both commander and troops who had seemed able to ride out every offensive of the 8th Army and come back fighting.

By the time of the Second Battle of Alamein Rommel was a sick man. When the offensive broke, he was in hospital at Zemmering in Germany, and was ordered to Africa to take over from General Stumme, who had died of a heart attack.

There was little Rommel could do. General Montgomery had taken time to build up a massive superiority of *matériel*, and preceded the attack with a crushing artillery barrage.

The retreat along the coast was masterly, but mines and local counter-attacks were of little value when the Allies landed in Morocco and Algeria. It was left to Rommel to give one more demonstration of his offensive flair when he fell upon the American troops newly arrived in Africa, and tore into the U.S. II Corps.

Recalled to Italy, and then transferred to France, Rommel was given the task of preparing the coasts of *Festung Europa* against Allied attack. Once more the energy that had shaped the barriers of mines and fixed emplacements at Alamein was brought to bear, but this time on coastal defences. "Sweat saves blood" was a proverb he drummed into garrisons, and the carnage at Omaha beach in 1944 showed how his orders had been obeyed.

On July 17, 1944 his car was caught by ground strafing fighters and he was badly wounded. Invalided home, his name was linked with the bomb attempt on Hitler's life on July 20. On October 14, faced with the choice of a show trial in a "Peoples Court", or suicide by poison, he chose the latter. Although Hitler had virtually blackmailed Rommel into committing suicide the dead Field-Marshal was given a full-dress state funeral befitting one of Germany's greatest heroes, with messages of sympathy from Hitler, Goebbels, and Ribbentrop cynically lamenting his death.

6

3. *Rommel pauses in a briefing to consult General Cruewell (right) commander of the* Afrika Korps. *On the left is Colonel Fritz Bayerlein, Cruewell's chief of staff.*

4. *On one of his constant visits to the front Rommel meets Major the Rev. (Pappa Willi) Bach, defender of Halfaya Pass. "During his visits to the front he saw everything . . .when a gun was inadequately camouflaged, when mines were laid in insufficient number, or when a standing patrol did not have enough ammunition, Rommel would see to it."*

5. *Kesselring and Rommel, with Crüwell. Kesselring's desert air force provided ground attack and air cover, but the relationship between the commanders varied with the fortunes of war.*

6. *With Italian officers Rommel inspects the first German troops to land in North Africa. In his journal he commented: "They radiated complete assurance of victory, and the change of atmosphere did not pass unnoticed in Tripoli."*

7. *A general and his maps. In attack he was flexible, and his tendency to lead from the front often meant that he was not available at his headquarters, where the overall conduct of operations would be left to his staff.*

8. *Rommel's sketch on which he plotted the British attack, on November 20, intended to relieve Tobruk.*

9. *The drive to the Canal: the map on which Rommel plotted his proposed moves should he break through after the battle of Alam Halfa. With no pontoon bridging equipment in North Africa, he planned to capture the Nile bridges by* coup-de-main.

7

8

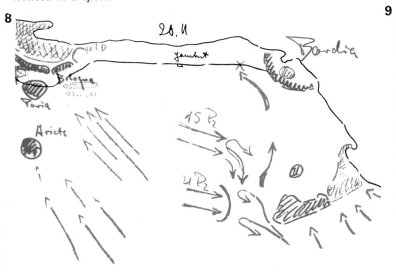

9

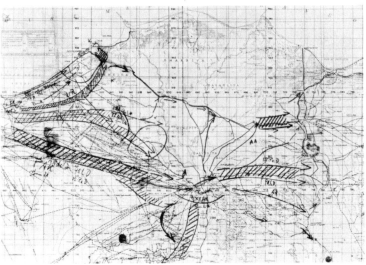

CHAPTER 63
Malta Survives

The successes of the Axis forces in Cyrenaica resounded like a thunderclap on the banks of the Thames. On January 25, the Prime Minister, "much disturbed" by the report that the 8th Army was intending to evacuate Benghazi and Derna, cabled General Auchinleck:

"It seems to me this is a serious crisis, and one to me quite unexpected. Why should they all be off so quickly? Why should the 4th (British-) Indian Division not hold out at Benghazi, like the Huns at Halfaya? The kind of retirement now evidently envisaged by subordinate officers implies the failure of 'Crusader' and the ruin of 'Acrobat'." In his memoirs, Churchill says that he refused to accept General Auchinleck's explanation that the "only" reason for this defeat, which was "so serious and heavy with consequences", had been the mechanical unreliability of the British armour about which Auchinleck had complained previously. Certainly the opinion may be allowed, but no one could deny that this very real inferiority of the British tanks compared with the Panzers weighed heavily in the balance. But again, what so irritated the Prime Minister in the event was not only that "Acrobat" (the advance on Tripoli) had to be postponed, but that there was also now the greater danger to Malta after the 8th Army's retreat to the Gazala–Bir Hakeim line, and this at a time when the Luftwaffe's II and X *Fliegerkorps* and the Italian Air Force were pounding the island.

From the airstrips in the Benghazi area, some 420 miles from Valletta, or, at a pinch, from Derna (530 miles), the R.A.F. could give continuous support to convoys from Alexandria supplying the beleaguered island. This was impossible from Tobruk (580 miles) and, to make matters worse, the "bump" of Cyrenaica, retaken by Rommel, was only 190 miles from Crete. The seas between were thus at the mercy of Axis cross-fire. Nevertheless, in January Admiral Cunningham succeeded in getting through to Malta three merchant ships and the supply-ship *Breconshire* for the loss of only one vessel. But February's convoy was a total failure: out of three merchant ships which left Alexandria, one had to be sent in to Tobruk because of the damage caused by enemy bombs, a second was sunk, and the third had to be scuttled.

The second battle of Sirte

Admiral Cunningham could not abandon Malta to her dire fate. He therefore organised another convoy of three merchant ships and the supply-ship *Breconshire*, which had meanwhile returned from Valletta. Rear-Admiral Philip Vian, of *Altmark* fame, who had commanded the previous convoys, was put in charge of this risky operation and, on March 20 he set sail from Alexandria with an escort of four light cruisers, ten destroyers, and six *Hunt*-class destroyer escorts. At dawn on the 22nd he was joined by the cruiser *Penelope* and the destroyer *Legion* which had come out from Malta to bring the merchant ships in. But Vian's movements had been spotted off Derna by the Italian

The two sides of the desperate air battle for Malta.
◄ *Takali airfield, to the west of Valletta, after the Axis raid of April 29, 1942. The white spots each indicate a bomb crater on the airfield itself and the dispersal areas around it. The angular constructions around the perimeter are blast pens for aircraft on the ground.*
▽ *Castel Vetrano airfield in Sicily, photographed by an R.A.F. reconnaissance aircraft on January 3, 1942. There are between 70 and 80 aircraft to be seen, mostly torpedo bombers and transport machines.*

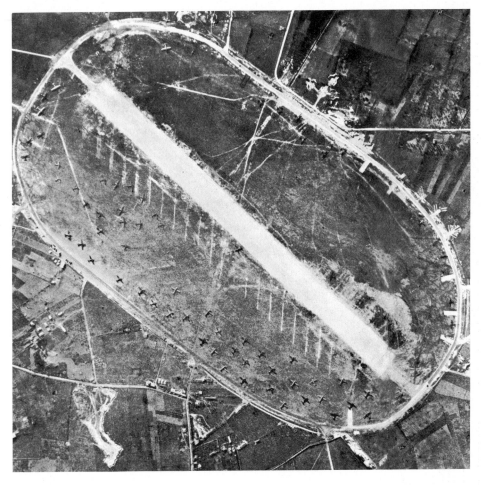

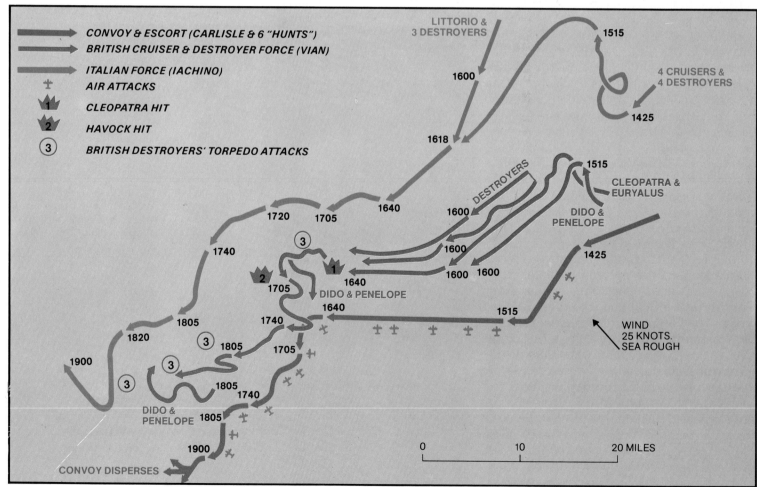

LITTORIO &
3 DESTROYERS
1515

1600

4 CRUISERS &
4 DESTROYERS

1425

1618

CONVOY & ESCORT (CARLISLE & 6 "HUNTS")
BRITISH CRUISER & DESTROYER FORCE (VIAN)
ITALIAN FORCE (IACHINO)
AIR ATTACKS
1 CLEOPATRA HIT
2 HAVOCK HIT
3 BRITISH DESTROYERS' TORPEDO ATTACKS

DESTROYERS

1515
CLEOPATRA &
EURYALUS

1600

1600

DIDO &
PENELOPE

1720   1705   1640

1600   1600   1425

1740

3

1600   1600

2   1
1705   1640

1805   1740   1640

1515

1820

3

1805

1705

DIDO & PENELOPE

WIND
25 KNOTS.
SEA ROUGH

1900   3

3   1805

1740

DIDO &
PENELOPE   1805

1900

CONVOY DISPERSES

0   10   20 MILES

860

submarine *Platino* and at midnight on the 21st the battleship *Littorio*, flying the flag of Admiral Iachino, sailed from Taranto, whilst an hour later the cruisers *Gorizia*, *Trento*, and *Bande Nere* left Messina. Each of these two detachments was escorted by four destroyers. At 1427 hours Rear-Admiral Parona's three cruisers made contact with the enemy, whereupon Vian made his convoy turn south-west, entrusting it to the A.A. guns of the old cruiser *Carlisle* and the *Hunts*, and engaged the Italians with the rest of his forces. The Italians would not join battle, but preferred to await the arrival of the battleship *Littorio*, which appeared on the scene towards 1640 hours.

Admiral Iachino's plan was to get between Malta and the convoy and then wipe out the ships, but the sirocco, blowing in gusts from the south-east, allowed Vian to take cover behind a smoke-screen, which the Italians, having no radar, could not penetrate. When one of the British cruisers did appear out of the smoke, the enemy could not engage it because of the spray and the smoke which obscured their range-finders. Thus the Italians' enormous superiority in fire-power was of little avail to them. At nightfall Iachino made a last attempt to get near to the convoy but he had to withdraw, driven off by the volleys of torpedoes fired off at him by the British destroyers as they counter-attacked and, as none of his ships was equipped for night-fighting, he had to abandon the action a little before 1900 hours.

The result of this second battle of Sirte was not as disappointing for the Italians as it might at first have seemed. Admiral Cunningham had lost the destroyers *Havock* and *Kingston*, which had been heavily damaged and had had to make for Malta. The convoy, having had to sail south-west for hours, could not now reach Valletta before dawn on the 23rd. This caused the loss by bombing of the *Breconshire* and one merchant ship: the two survivors reached harbour but were sunk as they were unloading. And so, out of the 26,000 tons of supplies which had left Alexandria only 5,000 reached their destination. On the other hand two Italian destroyers, ploughing on through the storm, sank with most of their crews. The light cruiser *Bande Nere* was so severely damaged in the same storm that she had to be sent to La Spezia for repairs. On the way there she was sunk by the submarine *Urge* (Lieutenant-Commander E. P. Tomkinson). This was a compensation for the loss of the light cruiser *Naiad*, which had gone down under Rear-Admiral Vian on February 11 in the previous year, torpedoed off the coast of Egypt by U-*565*.

The tragic situation of Malta

The bombardment of Malta, which had been intensified from mid-December 1941 to the end of February, became in March a veritable ordeal by fire: in 31 days 4,927 bombing sorties were flown against the island, and in April no fewer than 9,599 dropped 6,700 tons of bombs. In the Grand Harbour three destroyers, including *Kingston* were sunk and the valiant *Penelope* was so riddled with shrapnel that her crew facetiously renamed her *Pepperpot*. To avoid destruction, the submarines of the 10th Flotilla had to submerge by day with reduced crews.

For its part, the island's air force was decimated in battles in the air or wiped out on the ground. On January 31 there were only 28 fighters left; a fortnight later, there were only 11. In this almost desperate situation help came from the west, that is from Force H, now commanded by Rear-Admiral E. N. Syfret who had taken over from Sir James Somerville. On March 6 the old *Argus*, the first "flat-top" of any navy in the world, and the *Eagle* sent 15 Spitfires, more capable than the Hurricanes of dealing with the Messerschmitt Bf 109F's of X *Fliegerkorps*. This operation was successfully repeated on March 21 and 29.

Generous gesture by America

To speed up the reinforcement of Malta's defence, Winston Churchill appealed to President Roosevelt. On April 1, after describing the tragic situation of Malta's defenders, who had only 20 to 30 fighters as against the 600 of the Axis, and the difficulties of sending them enough Spitfires on the carriers at his disposal, he added:

"Would you be willing to allow your carrier *Wasp* to do one of these trips provided details are satisfactorily agreed between the Naval Staffs? With her broad lifts, capacity and length, we

▽ *Rear-Admiral Sir Philip Vian, commanding the 15th Cruiser Squadron. He had first hit the headlines in the* Altmark *incident, and was now displaying the same panache and initiative in the Mediterranean.*

△ ◁ *"The Convoy led by Admiral Vian fighting its way through to Malta, 1942" by Charles Pears. Just such an occasion led to the 2nd Battle of Sirte. On the left is the Italian force, with the British light cruisers and destroyers heading towards them in the centre of the painting, while the convoy tries to make its escape at the right.*
▽ ◁ *The 2nd Battle of Sirte. Once again, inferior British forces, though inferior in fire-power, held their own against superior Italian forces thanks to skilful handling and correct use of the prevailing weather conditions.*

The British light cruiser *Penelope*

Displacement: 5,270 tons.
Armament: six 6-inch, eight 4-inch A.A., eight 2-pdr A.A., and eight .5-inch machine guns, plus six 21-inch torpedo tubes and one aircraft.
Armour: 2-inch belt and deck, 1-inch turrets and director control tower.
Speed: $32\frac{1}{4}$ knots.
Length: 506 feet.
Beam: 51 feet.
Draught: $13\frac{3}{4}$ feet.
Complement: 450.

The Italian battleship *Littorio*

Displacement: 41,377 tons.
Armament: nine 15-inch, twelve 6-inch, twelve 3.5-inch A.A., twenty 37-mm A.A., and twenty-eight to thirty-two 20-mm A.A. guns, plus three aircraft.
Armour: 14-inch belt and turrets, $10\frac{1}{4}$-inch control tower, and $8\frac{1}{4}$-inch deck.
Speed: 28 knots.
Length: 782 feet.
Beam: 108 feet.
Draught: $31\frac{1}{2}$ feet.
Complement: 1,861.

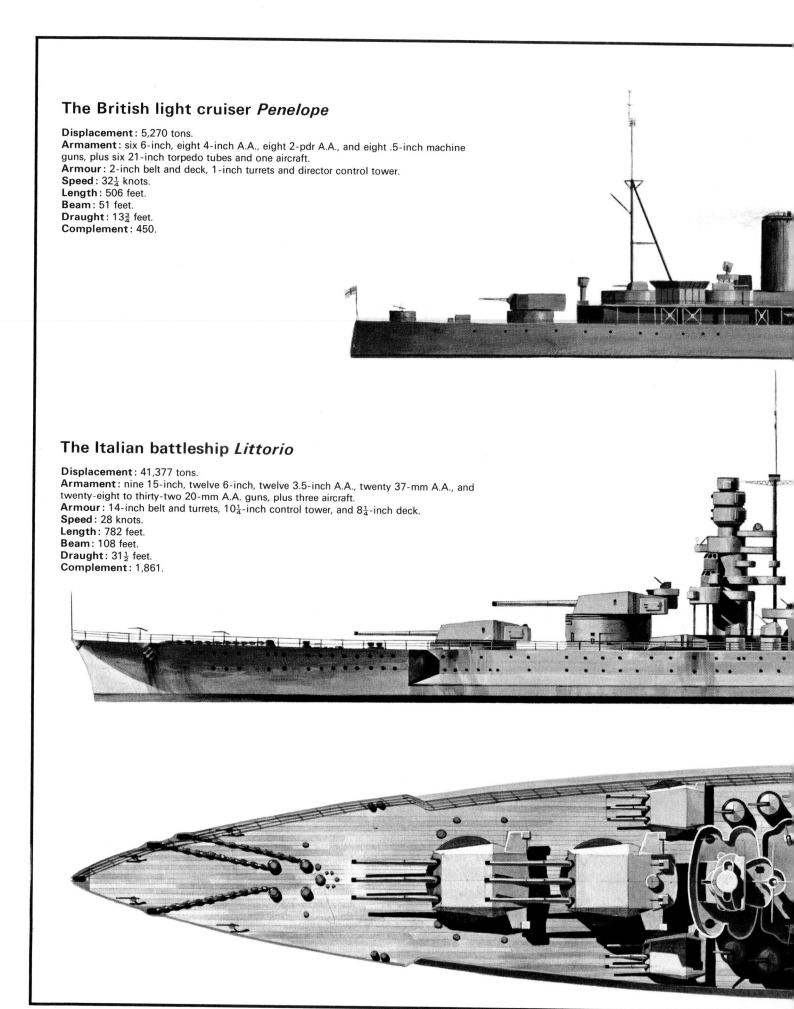

estimate that *Wasp* could take 50 or more Spitfires. Unless it were necessary for her to fuel, *Wasp* could proceed through the Straits at night without calling at Gibraltar until on the return journey, as the Spitfires would be embarked in the Clyde. Thus, instead of not being able to give Malta any further Spitfires during April, a powerful Spitfire force could be flown into Malta at a stroke and give us a chance of inflicting a very severe and possibly decisive check on the enemy. Operation might take place during third week of April."

President Roosevelt responded to his ally's request in a fine spirit of comradeship. Thus on April 20 *Wasp*, which had got within 620 miles of Malta, sent off 47 Spitfires; these were reduced to six four days later after redoubled attacks by the Luftwaffe. Churchill had therefore to ask for a second run by the American aircraft-carrier and he did this with an argument worth mentioning. He cabled the President on April 20:

"Without this aid I fear Malta will be pounded to bits. Meanwhile its defence is wearing out the enemy's Air Force and effectively aiding Russia."

Roosevelt responded again with help and *Wasp* went back into the Mediterranean on May 9. Together with *Eagle* she sent off 64 Spitfires to Malta; these were followed by a further 17 on May 15 from the British carrier alone. Churchill relates in his memoirs:

"It may be well here to complete the story of the *Wasp*. On May 9 she successfully delivered another important flight of Spitfires to struggling Malta. I made her a signal: 'Who said a wasp couldn't sting twice?' The *Wasp* thanked me for my 'gracious' message. Alas, poor *Wasp*! She left the dangerous Mediterranean for the Pacific and on September 15 was sunk by Japanese torpedoes. Happily her gallant crew were saved. They had been a link in our chain of causation."

The fact remains, however, that the population and the garrison of the island-fortress were put on short rations and that their supply of flour was due to run out on about June 15.

Axis plans against Malta

For a long time now Grand-Admiral Raeder had been maintaining to the Führer that the war would be won at Suez and Basra, but that the capture of these two objectives depended on the seizure of Malta. The day after Admiral Ciliax had forced a passage through the Straits of Dover, Hitler was somewhat more receptive to these ideas and, at the end of February, Field-Marshal Kesselring could write to Marshal Cavallero without fear of repudiation:

"The Führer is in complete agreement with the Italian Command for definite action against the island of Malta. He is following the development of this action with great interest; he will give it all possible support unless Britain attempts a landing on such a scale that it would require a maximum concentration of our forces."

And a few days later, Keitel, the Chief-of-Staff of O.K.W., wrote along the same lines to his Italian opposite number, who welcomed the news as he had long been in favour of this operation, which he considered risky but necessary. Hence on April 12 a Planning H.Q. was set up under General Fassi. The two dictators met on April 30 at Klessheim near Salzburg, and Cavallero, warmly supported by Kesselring, put forward his plan. This produced no practical or theoretical objections, Hitler merely remarking that "an operation like this must be planned down to the smallest detail for if it fails there can be no going back to the beginning." On this agreement and the promise of substantial German support, the Chief-of-Staff of the *Comando Supremo* drew up his plan for a simultaneous attack on the islands of Malta and Gozo by:

1. Naval and air forces consisting of:
   a. 1,506 combat planes, including 666 from the Luftwaffe;
   b. Admiral Iachino's naval forces;
   c. Admiral Tur's 12th Naval Division (with all the means for landing); and
   d. 14 groups of submarines.
2. Land forces, under General Vecchiarelli, consisting of:
   a. the Luftwaffe's XI *Fliegerkorps* (General Student), a German parachute division, the "Folgore" parachute division, and the "Spezia" airborne division;
   b. XVI Corps (General Carlo Rossi), the "Assieta" Division and the "Napoli" Division; and
   c. XXX Corps (General Sogno), the "Superga", "Livorno", and "Friuli" Divisions.

△ *The American aircraft-carrier* Wasp (top), *and British* Argus. *Between them and the British* Eagle, *these two ships were largely instrumental in saving Malta by supplying her with fighter reinforcements.*

△ A heavily-laden Spitfire with a large "slipper"-type drop tank under its fuselage, roars down the flight deck of the carrier Eagle. On March 7, Eagle flew off 15 Spitfires, all flown by R.A.F. pilots having their first experience of carrier operations. All 15 aircraft reached Malta safely.

The operation was called "Herkules" by the Germans. They also contributed a number of heavy tanks and some 300 transport aircraft. The Axis powers would thus have eight divisions against the Allies' garrison on the two islands of 30,000–35,000 men under Lieutenant-General Sir William Dobbie.

It had been originally planned that the assault on Malta should precede Rommel's offensive. This was to start from the line Sollum–Halfaya–Sidi Omar. The need to train the "Folgore" Division paratroopers, however, compelled Cavallero to reverse this order of priority and the resultant delay was to have incalculable consequences.

General Carboni's opposition

Had Operation "Herkules", which the Italians called Esigenza "C3", any chance of success? The Duce's Chief-of-Staff did not doubt it, nor did Kesselring and Admiral Weichold, Raeder's liaison officer at Supermarina. On the other hand, at Leghorn, where he was conscientiously training the "Friuli" Division for its assault on the cliffs of Malta, General Giacomo Carboni considered that the enterprise was some new folly imposed on Italy by the Germans because of the servility of Cavallero. Nor did he keep this opinion to himself. In particular he spoke to Count Ciano of his pessimistic conclusions. Ciano often went to the great Tuscan port and Carboni had become friendly with him.

"I had a long and interesting conversation with Carboni," Ciano noted in his diary on May 31. "At the moment he is commanding one of the assault divisions which is to participate in the Malta operation. He is decidedly against it. He is convinced that we shall have heavy losses and that nothing will come of it. He takes it out on Cavallero, whom he considers to be an intriguer and a man of bad faith. He is also very pessimistic about the Russian Front. He doesn't think that the Germans can undertake any operations of far-reaching proportions during the summer. It is a war of position rather than anything else. From this he draws the most sinister conclusions about the German future. Carboni is a general of great ability. One must not forget, however, that he was dismissed by the Secret Military Intelligence for his anti-German attitude, and that he is the son of an American mother."

It was the same story again on June 20.

"General Carboni has come to Rome to talk over the Malta enterprise, which is set for the next new moon. He is convinced, technically convinced, that we are heading for an unheard-of disaster. Preparations have been childish, equipment is lacking and inadequate. The landing troops will never succeed in landing, or, if they land they are doomed to total destruction. All the commanders are convinced of this, but no one dares to speak for fear of reprisals by Cavallero."

But the commander of the "Friuli" Division went further than these talks with Ciano in what he calls his "preparatory fire against the General Staff". He did not hesitate, in fact, to inform the Prince of Piedmont of his misgivings. The Prince, as the relevant army group C.-in-C. had been called upon to supervise the operation. The memorandum sent to him by Carboni late in May 1942 covers two pages in the Prince's memoirs and we will give the reader only the introduction and the conclusion:

"The Malta operation, carried out with the inadequate means at our disposal, takes on the appearance of a new folly, the consequences of which will be not only a new loss of military and political prestige to us and an irreparable loss of men, ships, and planes but will also have another effect.

"There is reason to fear that the enemy might take advantage of a defeat on Malta by landing in Italy and that our ally might seize on this 'new confirmation of our strategic and tactical weakness' to take over command and ravage our country. And so the Malta expedition will be in every way profitable to the Germans. It has certain similarities with the operation at Sidi Barrani in the sense that it might have the same consequences for our country as Sidi Barrani had for Libya: it would bring the British or the Germans here, and perhaps both of them together."

Pessimist or realist?

After the heir to the throne, General Carboni approached the King himself during a royal inspection of his division, but apparently without any more success. The fact remains, however, that these complaints, which were not made through the proper channels, brought no sanctions on their author, though General Ambrosio, the Army Chief-of-Staff, was not unaware of them. Not only did General Carboni remain in command of the "Friuli" Division but in December 1942 he was appointed commander of the corps occupying Corsica. *Esigenza "C3"*

△ *Spitfire V's on a Malta airfield. All too soon, however, the overwhelming numerical superiority enjoyed by the Axis whittled away the reinforcements flown in from the carriers.*

▽ *April 24, 1942, and thick palls of dust from Malta's light soil drift over Floriana, south-west of Valletta, in the aftermath of a raid. The twin-spired church is St. Publius, badly damaged in the raids of April.*

▽ *The desperate condition of Malta meant that all useful hands were turned to the work in hand. Here soldiers make up ammunition belts for the 20-mm wing cannon of Spitfires.*
▽▽ *A pilot waits in his cockpit as soldiers and airmen refuel and rearm his Spitfire in its dispersal pen.*

was cancelled for reasons which we shall examine later. It is naturally difficult to decide who would have been right, Cavallero or Carboni, the optimist or the pessimist. There are, however, two observations to be made on this controversy:

1. That the Malta undertaking was not in any way imposed on the Chief-of-Staff of the *Comando Supremo* by the Germans, as the former commander of the "Friuli" Division states. From the beginning to the end of this affair, all the initiatives point to Cavallero rather than to O.K.W. It would seem that those concerned were only too glad to take advantage of Rommel's victories to climb down from the undertakings that had been made; and

2. It cannot be denied that the means at the disposal of General Vecchiarelli were "inadequate" for the execution of his mission, at least to some extent. But Carboni in his argument makes no allusion to the state in which a surprise

attack might have found the defenders. Neither General Dobbie on the spot nor the Chiefs-of-Staff Committee in London were very optimistic about holding Malta without a prompt and vigorous offensive by the 8th Army.

As we have quoted Count Ciano and General Carboni, witnesses for the prosecution in this historic dispute, it is only right that we should hear the witness for the defence, Admiral Vittorio Tur who, it will be remembered, had been put in charge of the landing operations proper. He wrote of Marshal Cavallero:

"I can state that the Marshal was a true leader for whom I had the highest esteem and devotion and whose end showed the firmness of his character and the uprightness of his conscience; a leader who always encouraged and appreciated the preparatory work which had been done, giving sound advice and intelligent orders, and who never had the slightest doubt about the outcome of the operation."

CHAPTER 64
Breakthrough at Gazala

These considerations naturally bring us to Operation "Venezia", started by Rommel in the evening of May 26, 1942. It was no doubt going to set the seal on his indisputable tactical genius, but it was also to show, by the way in which he went too far in insisting on freedom of action, a certain incapacity on his part to rise to the level of a total conception of warfare and to sacrifice to this his own initiative. The reverse also deserves consideration, however: that is, if *Comando Supremo* did not manage to impose on Rommel the strategic zig-zag of Tobruk–Malta–Tobruk–Suez which it wanted, it was because it did not have the tactical means of forcing its will on its German ally. Finally the double subordination of the

Panzerarmee Afrika to both *Comando Supremo* and the *Oberkommando der Wehrmacht* made it easy for its commander to adopt the rôle of the lonely knight of destiny which, within four months, was to turn a resounding victory into an irreparable defeat.

The mobile forces of the Axis, having taken on their own initiative a position on the line Gulf of Bomba–Bir Temrad–Rotunda Segnali, could not be left to face alone the British 8th Army, which was regrouping and falling back on the line Aïn el-Gazala–Bir Hakeim. So Cavallero agreed to bring forward towards these mobile forces his X and XXI Corps and to put them, as the tactical corps troops (now XX Corps) already were, under the com-

△ *Rommel, always eager to keep his enemy on a retreating defensive towards the Suez Canal.*
▽ *A Pzkw IV ploughs on towards Gazala. The lack of opposition can be deduced from the exposed positions of the crew.*

mand of Colonel-General Rommel. To relieve the tension which had now become obvious between the latter and Marshal Bastico, the Italian C.-in-C. North Africa, he recalled General Gambara to Rome and replaced him by General Barbasetti di Prun as Chief-of-Staff in Tripoli.

As for the immediate future, the commander of the *Panzerarmee Afrika* was of the opinion that the enemy's preparations for a new offensive had to be forestalled, and on April 30 he submitted to Marshal Bastico, Field-Marshal Kesselring, Admiral Weichold, and *Comando Supremo* through Rintelen, an initial outline of his plans:

"The commander of the *Panzerarmee Afrika*, taking advantage of the balance of forces which is at present in our favour, intends to attack in the early days of June (the moon then being favourable) the British forces at present in the area Bir el Gubi–Tobruk–Aïn el-Gazala–Bir Hakeim and annihilate them. Following on this action he proposes also to take the garrison of Tobruk, by a surprise attack if possible."

An encircling movement by his motorised forces as they broke out on each side of Bir Hakeim towards Acroma would compel the enemy to fight on a reverse front and his complete defeat would be assured in the evening of the second day. Forty-eight hours should be enough to prepare the assault on Tobruk and Rommel could expect to be ready to advance on the Sollum–Bardia front on

about the sixth day. This attack should take place, in his opinion, after the taking of Malta, but if the Malta operation could not be launched before June 1 he might have to take the initiative: otherwise it would pass to the enemy.

Cavallero, who had gone to Cyrenaica on May 5, raised no objection to the plan submitted to him. On the contrary, he approved it in his directive dated that day, though placing it in the more general framework of operations in the Mediterranean theatre. Because of its intelligent assessment, it is worth quoting two points from this document:

"1. *Objective:* to defeat the enemy's mobile forces west of Tobruk. If outcome successful, prompt attack on Tobruk.

"Capture of Tobruk is categorical condition for advance of our forces; if this condition fulfilled, we advance to the line Sollum–Halfaya–Sidi Omar which the main body of the armour must not pass. If the occupation of Tobruk is not successful, the objective after the battle will not be beyond the Gazala line . . .

"4. *Time available for the operation.* Operations cannot continue beyond June 20 since by this date the supporting air and naval units at present in Cyrenaica will have to be withdrawn, all of them being destined for other use by this date. A resumption of operations must be expected in the autumn."

As he explained in his diary, the Duce's Chief-of-Staff wanted to avoid involving the Axis forces in a war of attrition such as they had had to fight the previous year when they had to maintain at the same time the siege of Tobruk and their frontier positions. But he wrote in particular:

"The operations in Marmarica must not compromise the preparation and the execution of *Esigenza "C3"* [Malta] which is essential for the later development of the war in the Mediterranean."

So it was important for the air detachments in Cyrenaica to be sent back to Sicily and prepared for further action. Rommel was limited by both time and space. In acting thus, Cavallero was obeying considerations of a strategic nature, which he had explained to Field-Marshal Kesselring on March 18 in the following terms:

"After the capture of Tobruk there must be absolutely no further advance. There must be a break. Tobruk–the Nile: it's only a dream."

It is odd that these documents are not mentioned at all in the papers Rommel left behind; indeed there is a gap from April 28 to May 12, 1942. But it is clear that the commander of the *Panzerarmee Afrika* had received clear and sensible orders from *Comando Supremo* and that he was wrong to ignore them.

Churchill urges Auchinleck to go over to the offensive

In London, meanwhile, the Prime Minister was getting more and more irritated at General Auchinleck's reluctance to launch an offensive. As far back as February 26 he had taken him to task over this, evidencing the supposed superiority of the 8th Army in tanks, planes, and other weapons. Cairo disputed this and claimed that no operation on any worthwhile scale could be started before June 1, although it was proposed to strengthen as much as possible the line from Gazala to Bir Hakeim, extend the Marsa Matrûh railway down to El Adem, south of Tobruk, build up an armoured striking force, establish more forward ordnance depôts and, if the situation warranted it, make a limited attack to recover the airstrips in the Derna–Mechili area. This programme was not to Churchill's liking, and on March 8 he sent a message to summon the British C.-in-C. Middle East to London to confer with him about the situation. When the latter refused, he

The British 6-pounder anti-tank gun.
It had been realised as early as 1938 that the 2-pounder anti-tank gun then in service would need replacing by a more powerful weapon, and design work was initiated on a new gun, the 6-pounder. The gun was not, however, put into production for fear of disrupting the delivery of 2-pounders. But the need for a heavier weapon received higher priority in 1940, and tests on the 6-pounder showed it to be an excellent weapon. Production was ordered in June, but it was not until November that it got under way, though at a quickly-rising tempo. In April 1942, 1,500 guns were produced. The following specifications are for the 6-pounder Mark II. Weight in action: 2,740 lbs. Crew: five. Weight of armour-piercing shot: 6.25 lbs. Muzzle velocity: 2,675 feet per second. Range: 5,500 yards. Armour penetration at an impact angle of 30°: 79-mm at 500 yards, 72-mm at 750 yards, 65-mm at 1,000 yards, and 52-mm at 1,500 yards. It should be noted that if the shot hit armour at short range and at right angles, its penetration would be about a quarter as much again. At 60° it would be slightly under half the figure given for 30°.

took up his pen again on the 15th and wrote him a long letter, of which we quote the fourth and last paragraph:

"4. I have done everything in my power to give you continuous support at heavy cost to the whole war. It would give me the greatest pain to feel that mutual understanding had ceased. In order to avoid this, I have asked Sir Stafford Cripps to stop for a day in Cairo about 19th or 20th on his way to India, and put before you the views of the War Cabinet. He will be joined by General Nye, who is proceeding separately, and is fully possessed of the Chiefs of Staff's opinion."

But to the Prime Minister's great displeasure both the Lord Privy Seal and Sir Archibald Nye were won over to Auchinleck's view, which also had the support of Air Chief-Marshal Tedder. Both had to agree that neither the situation in the air nor the performance of the tanks could guarantee the success of any large-scale offensive operation for the moment. Perhaps the canny Scot Auchinleck might have been thought to have pulled the wool over the eyes of the civilian Sir Stafford Cripps; if so, he could hardly have done the same with Lieutenant-General Nye, an experienced military man and, moreover, Deputy C.I.G.S. The latter nevertheless got a most disagreeable letter, to say the least, from Churchill:

"I have heard from the Lord Privy Seal. I do not wonder everything was so pleasant, considering you seem to have accepted everything they said, and all *we* have got to accept is the probable loss of Malta and the Army standing idle, while the Russians are resisting the German counter-stroke desperately, and while the enemy is reinforcing himself in Libya faster than we are."

This debate, which died down for a time, flared up again at the beginning of May when Auchinleck asked for further delays and was nearly relieved of his command. As chairman of the Chiefs-of-Staff Committee, Brooke poured floods of oil on the troubled waters at Downing Street. But, although he could normally be very severe on the Prime Minister's strategic improvisations, he did not necessarily agree with everyone who contradicted Churchill, and on this occasion he thought that Auchinleck had "once more put his foot in it."

On May 10 he noted:

"We framed a proposed policy at C.O.S. in which we laid down that we considered that the value of Malta was underestimated, whilst his argument against attack was not very convincing. Finally we suggested that he should be allowed to wait to take advantage of possible limited German offensive for Tobruk to put in a counter-stroke, but that the June convoy

▽ *An Italian anti-tank gun crew rushes to bring its weapon into action. As can be imagined, in theatres like North Africa, the general scarcity of cover placed a premium on the incorporation of a low silhouette into the design of anti-tank guns, which had to engage the enemy at short ranges.*

△ △ *British Infantry Tanks Mark III, Valentines, on manoeuvres. Unlike most British tanks, the Valentine had been designed as a private venture by Vickers, rather than to a War Office specification. Mechanically, the Valentine was based on the Cruiser Tanks Marks I and II, and was ordered straight into production in the middle of 1939. By the time production ceased in early 1944, 8,275 had been built. The Valentine entered service with the 8th Army in 1941, and because there was a shortage of Cruisers, had to serve in this capacity as well as its designed role of Infantry Tank.*

△ *A lesson that could not be repeated too often: poor workmanship cost lives.*

to Malta should be the latest date, as this afforded the last opportunity of assisting in the supply of Malta."

The members of the War Cabinet, questioned individually by Churchill on the proposals of the Chiefs-of-Staff, approved them unanimously and G.H.Q. Cairo henceforth made no further objections.

In fact, on May 27 Ritchie had some 994 tanks, compared with Rommel's 560. On both sides of the balance-sheet there were non-starters to be deducted (Italian M13's, German Pzkw II's, British Matildas, Valentines, and Crusaders), giving a slight advantage to the *Panzerwaffe*. Rommel had 232 Pzkw III's and 38 Pzkw IV's with respectively 5- and 7.5-cm guns and against them were only 160 M3 Grants, the only tanks which could match them. This American tank had a 75-mm gun with a longer range than the Pzkw IV's 7.5-cm weapon. The Grant was very similar to the French B1 *bis* but its gun was mounted in a casemate on the driver's right, which greatly restricted its field of fire–the whole tank had to be aimed by means of its tracks whenever the enemy appeared even marginally on its left. Its high silhouette made it visible from some distance by the low-slung Panzers, whose turret-mounted guns were capable of all-round fire.

This was not all, however: the new 6-pounder anti-tank gun with which the British infantry were being re-equipped had only reached the 8th Army in

small numbers. The main anti-tank defence was still the 2-pdr gun, here and now declared to be outmatched by the 5-cm guns of the German tanks which, choosing their distance, could pick off the British like sitting ducks.

The 8th Army's air support, though numerically superior, was qualitatively inferior. The Messerschmitt Bf 109F's and G's were noticeably better than the British Hurricanes or the American Curtiss Warhawks and Kittyhawks. Moreover, the training of the Luftwaffe pilots seems to have been better than that of the R.A.F.'s, as shown by the 158 victims accredited to Captain Hans-Joachim Marseille, killed in an accident on September 30 over El Alamein. In these conditions, the Stukas could take up again their rôle of flying artillery without the R.A.F.'s bombers being able to get their own back on the armoured columns of the *Panzerarmee*.

These defects in British armour could be seen more clearly from Cairo than from London and justified Sir Claude Auchinleck's caution in face of Winston Churchill's fiery exhortations. But the development of the battle was going to reveal further weaknesses which the C.-in-C. British Forces in the Middle East was far from suspecting.

On May 27 the British 8th Army had six divisions and six brigades, which General Ritchie had deployed as follows:
1. XIII Corps, now under the command of Lieutenant-General W. H. E. Gott, had

its 1st South African Division (Pien- aar) blocking the Via Balbia opposite Gazala and its 50th Division (Ramsden) blocking the track running parallel to the coast road 18–19 miles further south; the 1st and 32nd Army Tank Brigades were in support with their 276 Matildas and Valentines.

In second echelon XIII Corps had the 2nd South African Division and the 9th Indian Brigade as the garrison of Tobruk; and

2. XXX Corps (Lieutenant-General C. Willoughby Norrie) had in its first line the 1st Free French Brigade occupying the base point of Bir Hakeim and the 3rd Indian Motorised Brigade extend- ing from this south-eastwards. The 1st and 7th Armoured Divisions (under Major-Generals Lumsden and Mes- servy respectively) were nine miles either side of "Knightsbridge", a focus of good tracks leading to Gazala, Sidi Muftah (50th Division), and Bir Hakeim. Finally, the 29th Indian Brigade had been withdrawn to Bir el Gubi.

Stretching from Gazala on the coast to the south of Bir Hakeim was an enormous minefield which ran round the French position and turned north up to the surroundings of Bir Harmat. Behind this obstacle XIII Corps' divisions had deploy- ed their brigades, reinforced by anti-tank weapons, A.A., and artillery in a number of all-round defence strongpoints. These dispositions did not entirely please Gener-

al Auchinleck. He would have liked XIII Corps to assume responsibility for the whole of the defensive front so that XXX Corps could devote itself entirely to its job of counter-attacking. In addition, he would have liked the 1st and 7th Armoured Divisions to close in on each other so that they could have been used as a single entity. But the advice which he gave to Ritchie along these lines was never put into the form of an order, and so was never acted upon.

On the opposing side Rommel divided his forces into two parts. Under the com- mand of General Cruewell, the Italian XXI Corps ("Trento" and "Sabratha" Divisions under Navarrini) and X Corps ("Pavia" and "Brescia" Divisions under Gioda), reinforced by some German units, would engage the 8th Army in a frontal attack to prevent its manoeuvring.

Rommel himself would have under his command the mobile forces of the Axis army, i.e. the Italian XX Corps ("Trieste" Motorised Division and "Ariete" Ar- moured Division under Baldassare) and the three divisions of the *Afrika Korps*: 15th and 21st Panzer, and 90th Light.

Rommel set out at dusk on May 26 on the outflanking attack which was to pass north and south of Bir Hakeim and take his tanks into the rear of the 8th Army. On his right the 90th Light Division was to make a feint towards El Adem, then turn back to Acroma and cut the Via Balbia, the enemy's last line of com- munication.

△ *An omen in the skies of North Africa. Certainly British troops and* matériel *were pouring into Egypt, but Rommel's genius and lack of British experience were still to deprive the 8th Army of its chance for a great victory–as yet.*

CHURCHILL
the ultimate "Man of War"?

Churchill's attitude to his task as Britain's war leader is summed up by one sentence in his memoirs: "I thought I knew a good deal about it all, and I was sure I should not fail." This comment is in fact one of the soundest keys to the way in which he chose to direct the British war effort.

There were three basic elements in Churchill's make-up. First came the experiences of his youth, when he had originally smelled powder on service in India, charged with the 21st Lancers against the Dervish army at Omdurman, and become a national hero by escaping from the clutches of the Boers in what is still a classic prisoner-of-war escapade.

He had been a man of action, and the zest for action never left him, whether it was reflected in braving shrapnel and Luftwaffe bombs during the Battle of Britain or pestering his generals to let him visit the front at inopportune or downright dangerous moments.

Second comes his experience as First Lord of the Admiralty between 1911 and 1915. During this period Churchill amassed a wealth of first-hand knowledge about how a fighting service is prepared for war and directed when war comes. His service to Britain in preparing the Grand Fleet for war in 1914 was surpassed only by his inspiring of the nation in 1940. Unfortunately

even in 1914 he "thought he knew a good deal about it all", and never stopped dreaming up ideas for using the Navy to break the deadlock on land. This has been condemned as "cigar-butt strategy"–pointing at the map and saying "let us do something there"–and it was always one of Churchill's biggest faults, causing endless wrangles with the generals, air marshals, and admirals who saw Churchill's schemes as distractions from the main objective.

There was, for example, Churchill's "Catherine" plan: to strip down two or three *Revenge*-class battleships and send them into the Baltic to wreak havoc

1. *A belligerent-looking Churchill in his sailor suit at the age of five, photographed in 1880.*
2. *Churchill as a Harrow schoolboy, taken about 1889.*
3. *The photograph of Churchill published by the Boers when he was on the run from prison camp – £25, dead or alive, for an Englishman "about 25 years old, about 5 feet 8 inches tall, indifferent build, walks with a forward stoop, pale appearance, reddish-brown hair, small and hardly-noticeable moustache, talks through his nose and cannot pronounce the letter 'S' properly."*
4. *Churchill, M.P., photographed in 1904 when he was 30 years old and Member for Oldham.*
5. *The men who forged the Grand Fleet: Churchill as First Lord of the Admiralty, an appointment he received in October 1911, with the dynamic First Sea Lord Admiral "Jacky" Fisher. Churchill's achievement at the Admiralty was summed up by Lord Kitchener when Churchill quitted his post after the Dardanelles fiasco in 1915: "One thing at any rate they cannot take from you: the Fleet was ready."*
6. *"Winston is back"–Churchill returns to the Admiralty as First Lord in September 1939.*

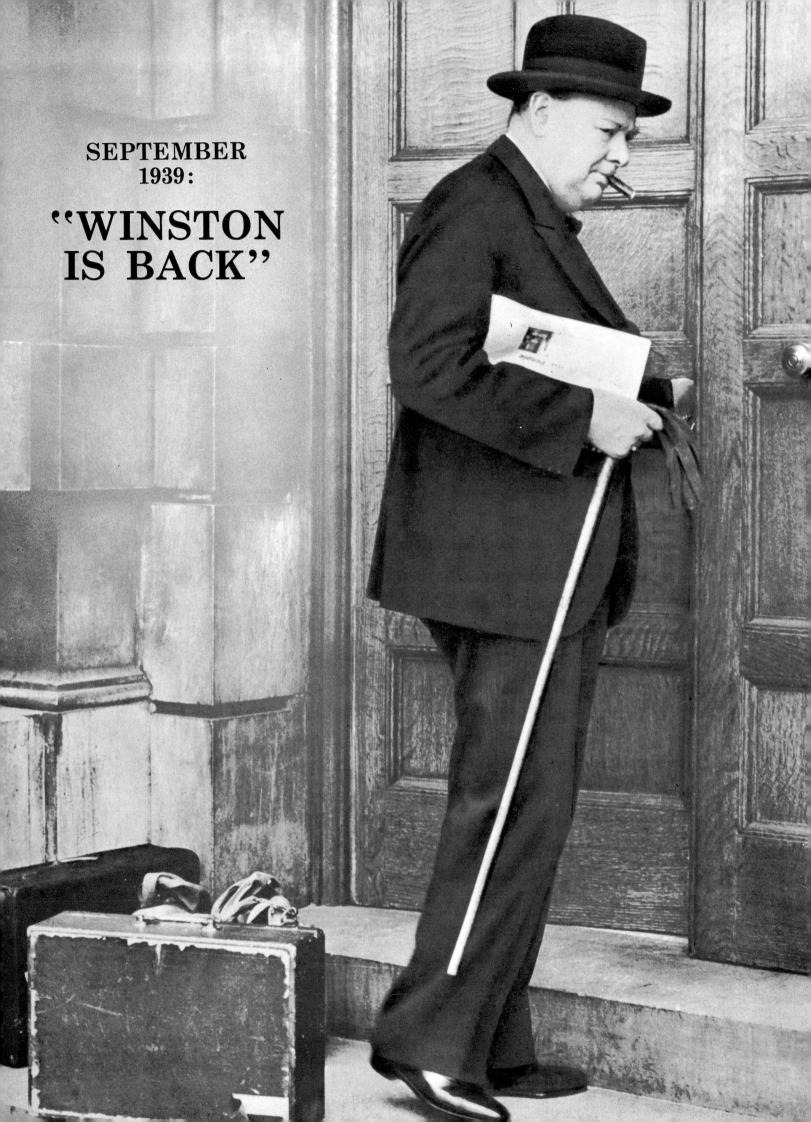

SEPTEMBER
1939:

"WINSTON
IS BACK"

7. First Lord Churchill addresses the men of H.M.S. Exeter after her hazardous return from the Falkland Islands. "In this sombre dark winter," he told his audience, "the brilliant action of the Plate . . . came like a flash of light and colour on the scene." Captain Bell, who commanded Exeter during the battle, is on Churchill's left.

8. Churchill with the First Sea Lord, Admiral Sir Dudley Pound. "I had strongly condemned in Parliament the dispositions of the Mediterranean Fleet when he commanded it, at the moment of the Italian descent on Albania. Now we met as colleagues . . . We eyed each other amicably if doubtfully. But from the earliest days our friendship and mutual confidence grew and ripened."

9. Hour of destiny. Churchill, now Prime Minister, broadcasts to the nation in his famous zip-front "siren suit".

10. Churchill with King George VI and Queen Elizabeth. "His Majesty received me most graciously and bade me sit down. He looked at me searchingly and quizzically for some moments, and then said: 'I suppose you don't know why I have sent for you?' Adopting his mood, I replied, 'Sir, I simply couldn't imagine why.' He laughed and said, 'I want to ask you to form a Government.' I said I would certainly do so."

11. Churchill broods over the blitzed ruins of the House of Commons.

along the Pomeranian coast. Later, after the Mediterranean campaign began, Churchill pressed Admiral Cunningham to sacrifice one of the more elderly battleships of the Mediterranean Fleet to block Tripoli harbour. Both these projects blithely forgot that the Navy needed every available capital ship to neutralise the German and Italian battle fleets, and they were very properly vetoed by the Navy chiefs.

Third, and most important for a war-time Prime Minister, Churchill had all the experience of four decades as a politician—"I am a child of the House of Commons." Only a seasoned politician of Churchill's stature could have handled the tricky task of smoothing out the inevitable differences arising from a coalition government, and of resisting popular pressure for votes of no confidence when things went wrong, not to mention the Left's never-ending cry of "Second Front Now".

These three aspects of Churchill's character were underlaid by his amazing energy. He travelled everywhere to see for himself—visiting gun batteries, coastal defences, bombed cities, criticising, inquiring, praising, irritating as often as not, but always inspiring. Nor was his constant desire to be the "man on the spot" limited to Britain. Compared with Stalin and Roosevelt, Churchill was certainly the most globe-trotting member of the "Big Three", and he usually contrived to get as close to the firing line as possible. (Only personal

intervention by the King stopped him from viewing the landings on D-Day from a Navy cruiser.)

This energy was also reflected in a passion for detail, which every great war leader has always had. (Comparing Hitler's concern for detail with that of Churchill is a fascinating pastime. In this respect they were virtually identical.) Thousands of minutes were written by Churchill, usually requesting information "on a half sheet of paper", and dealing with every subject under the sun from the performance of new weapons and units to the wording and distribution of "Most Secret" telegrams, or asking the Minister of War Transport about the ban on the transport of flowers by rail.

When it came to dealing with the generals and their prosecution of the war, Churchill's restless energy and constant desire for action at the earliest moment led him into deep waters. He hounded Wavell into the premature "Battleaxe" offensive and replaced him when it failed, and later replaced Auchinleck, victor of the first battle of Alamein, as well. On the other hand he wildly over-estimated the brilliant but unstable Wingate, hailing him as the T. E. Lawrence of World War II. And it is this aspect of Churchill as war leader which is most open to criticism.

A cynic would certainly have to admit that in at least one respect Churchill had learned much from his former contemporary, Lord Fisher: the ability to change his mind when circumstances dict-

12

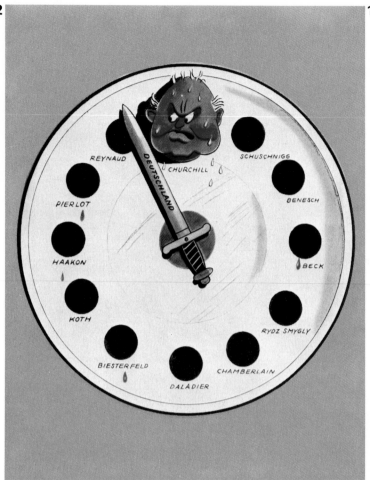

13

12. *Premature forecast: Berlin's* Lustige Blätter *sees the addition of Churchill to the list of fallen enemies of Germany as only a matter of time.*

13. *Marc' Aurelio of Rome depicts Churchill and Roosevelt indulging in mutual April foolery. "Let's take advantage of the date and give each other some good news, Delano . . ."*

14. *"Somewhere in the Atlantic", August 9, 1941: Churchill and Roosevelt meet for the first time. Roosevelt is supported by his son.*

15. *Stalin's Foreign Minister, Molotov, receives Churchill. During Churchill's visit to Moscow in August 1942,*

"Molotov drove me in his car to my appointed residence, eight miles out of Moscow, 'State Villa No. 7'. While going through the streets of Moscow, which seemed very empty, I lowered the window for a little more air, and to my surprise felt that the glass was over two inches thick. This surpassed all records in my experience. 'The Minister says it is more prudent,' said Interpreter Pavlov."

16. *Churchill visits the desert front. "Now for a short spell I became 'the man on the spot'. Instead of sitting at home waiting for the news I could send it myself. This was exhilarating."*

14

ated. His attitude to de Gaulle was a case in point. In 1940, with Reynaud's Cabinet on the verge of surrender, Churchill solemnly greeted de Gaulle as *"l'homme du destin"*. Three years later, when the prickly question of the figure-head of the Free French movement had become an acute embarrassment to one and all, Churchill was quoted as saying of de Gaulle "Oh, don't speak of him. We call him *Jeanne d'Arc* and we're looking for some bishops to burn him."

The same applied to Britain's sudden acquisition of Soviet Russia in the summer of 1941 as her most important ally. Since the Bolshevik Revolution of 1917 no man alive had been such an outspoken, committed critic of Communism as Churchill. He tackled the issue squarely, pointing out this very fact (and adding that "I will unsay no word that I have spoken about it.") Here again the parallel with Hitler was uncomfortably close. In his early days Hitler had stated quite baldly to his ministers that he was prepared to "sign anything". When he suddenly, unexpectedly, got Russia as an ally in the summer of 1941, Churchill commented "If Hitler invaded Hell I would at least make a favourable reference to the Devil in the **16** House of Commons" – and went on the air in typical vein. "I see the ten thousand villages of Russia where the means of existence is wrung so hardly from the soil, but where there are still primordial human joys, where maidens laugh and children play. I see advancing upon all this in hideous onslaught the Nazi war machine, with its clanking, heel-clicking, dandified Prussian officers, its crafty expert agents fresh from the cowing and tying down of a dozen countries. I see also the dull, drilled, docile, brutish masses of the Hun soldiery plodding on like a swarm of crawling locusts. I see the German bombers and fighters in the sky, still smarting from many a British whipping, delighted to find what they believe is an easier and a safer prey . . ."

Goebbels himself could not have done a better job. But Churchill went through with his pro-Russian drum-beating with open eyes. When the tide turned and the great German retreat in Russia began, he tried desperately to get Roosevelt to look ahead and put two and two together. Perhaps this was Churchill's biggest defeat. Roosevelt's great delusion was that he could "do

business with Joe". Churchill **15** saw things as they were. He was the man who had to take the brunt of Stalin's requests for help, first pleading, then insulting; and Churchill was never afraid to to speak his mind to the Russians. When M. Maisky came to him in September 1941, urging an immediate "Second Front" and an exorbitant monthly supply to Russia of 400 aircraft and 500 tanks, Churchill did not mince his words.

But on the other hand Churchill and Stalin were very alike, too. The worst piece of insolence Churchill ever had to take from Stalin – "Are you never going to start fighting? You will find it is not too bad if you once start!" – was no worse than some of the tart comments which Churchill dealt out to his own generals. And Churchill did not find it easy to be caught between pressure from Stalin and his own impulses.

Set against all the failings, however, are his determination, his energy, his political acumen, and his stature as the embodiment of the will to victory. Churchill did not delude himself. He did know a good deal about it all. And he did not fail.

The day of the 27th was for both sides an
inextricable mixture of successes and
reverses which left them uncertain of the
way the battle was going. On the right the
Afrika Korps overran the 3rd Indian
Motorised Brigade then routed the 7th
Armoured Division, whose two brigades
were caught, separated and unsupported,
by the 15th and 21st Panzer Divisions,
which attacked in close formation; even
so the German tanks were considerably
damaged by the Grants. On the left, however, XX Corps was completely stopped.
The "Trieste" Motorised Division slipped
out of Baldassare's control and was lost
but, more important, the "Ariete" Armoured Division was thrown back in front
of Bir Hakeim, losing 32 of its 163 tanks.
General Koenig, commanding the 1st Free
French Brigade, had had 50,000 mines laid
around his positions and also had 55 25-,
47-, and 75-mm anti-tank guns. In this trap
was captured, wounded, Colonel Prestissi-
mone, the commander of the Italian 132nd

Armoured Regiment; he was pulled out of
a tank, the third which he had had blown
up under him, evidence of the determination of the "Ariete" Armoured Division's
attack. At the end of the day, Rommel's
mobile forces, being counter-attacked
more and more closely by the British
XXX Corps, far from cutting the 8th
Army's communications, were finding
their own communications broken and
themselves trapped in minefields. And
the frontal attacks of the Italian X and
XXI Corps did not have the diversionary
effect the German commander expected.
On the whole, General Auchinleck in
Cairo and Winston Churchill in London
had every reason to be pleased, all the
more since on May 29 General Cruewell
had made a forced landing behind the
British lines and been captured.

But they were reckoning without Rommel. On May 28 his scouts had made contact with the forward elements of the
"Trieste" and "Pavia" Divisions and to-

Knightsbridge, linch pin of the southern part of the 8th Army's deployment. After Rommel's sweeping outflanking movement from the south and subsequent retreat into the "Cauldron", Knightsbridge became the concentration area for the British forces for the counter-attack into the "Cauldron" on June 5.

▽ *A lucky break for the British – General Cruewell, commander of the* Deutsches Afrika Korps *(extreme right), captured after his plane was forced down in May 1942.*

gether they made a narrow gap through the minefield, which restored communications, albeit precariously, with his rear areas. Then, covering himself in the "Knightsbridge" area against an attack from the British XXX Corps, he threw the mass of his armour against the strongpoint at Got el Oualeb, held by the left flank of the British 50th Division of XIII Corps. Caught also on their western flank by the Italian X Corps, the British 150th Brigade and the 1st Army Tank Brigade capitulated on June 2, yielding Rommel 3,000 prisoners, 124 guns, and 101 armoured vehicles.

The fall of Got el Oualeb opened a ten-mile wide gap in the minefield, allowing the *Panzerarmee Afrika* to reunite its forces and Rommel to regain the initiative. This he used to close the pincers round Bir Hakeim. As can be seen, the reaction of the British 8th Army had been slow and indecisive, and between May 29 and June 2 several occasions had arisen to exploit the risky situation into which the enemy had got himself, but these were purely and simply wasted. It would seem unjust to blame all this on General Ritchie. From all evidence his radio communications were bad and only gave him out-of-date news of the battle, but the Germans, combining with greater skill their tanks, infantry, anti-tank guns, and mines, were as inaccessible on the defensive as they were aggressive on the attack. Moreover, in a few days the 8th Army had lost 400 tanks, most of them Grants.

"The Cauldron"

And so the battle of what the British called "The Cauldron" was a fresh defeat for Ritchie. Skilfully laid minefields protected by batteries of 8.8-cm guns thwarted the most valiant attacks of the XIII and XXX Corps whose various units, unfortunately, were widely dispersed and sometimes out of contact one with the other. Then at a given point Rommel redoubled his armoured attack with the 15th Panzer and the 90th Light Divisions, which drove hard into the enemy's rear. As night fell on the "Knightsbridge" battlefield the Germans counted 4,000 prisoners, and the 32nd Tank Brigade alone had lost 50 out of the 70 tanks it had had at dawn.

In spite of this defeat, which robbed it of all hope of relief, the garrison at Bir Hakeim kept up its resistance under repeated bombing by Stukas and drove back the daily attacks of the 90th Light Division and the "Trieste" Motorised Division. General Koenig also had to cope with a delegation of Italian emissaries who got through to his command post to urge him to capitulate.

"On the stroke of 1030 hours," writes Jacques Mordal, "the officer commanding the 2nd Battalion of the Foreign Legion telephoned his Brigade Headquarters that a car flying a flag of truce was at the east gate. Two Italian officers got out and were led blindfolded to the General's headquarters by Captain de Sairigné. One of them said in Italian that he had come in the name of his own leader and in that of General Rommel, 'the great victor of Libya' to ask for a surrender so as to avoid useless bloodshed. . . . Was it not also in the interest of the defenders to be taken prisoner by the Italians, well known for their consideration, rather than to risk falling later into the hands of the Germans who would very likely show them little respect? . . . General Koenig did not seem impressed by the pertinence of this remark and merely replied very politely in French that there was absolutely no question of his surrendering. Upon this the two emissaries stood at attention and saluted. '*Grandi soldati*' they said as they withdrew."

Water and ammunition were running short and so the 1st Free French Brigade was ordered to evacuate the position it had so valiantly defended. More than 3,000 French, led by General Koenig,

reached the British lines during the course of the night June 10–11, leaving behind 984 missing, of whom 500 were taken prisoner.

Three nights later, when it was on the point of being surrounded, XIII Corps also disengaged. Ritchie's intention was to regroup to form a coherent force based on Tobruk. But he was reduced to 100 tanks and, slower than his adversary, he was driven back to the frontier and denied all contact with the fortress. This, moreover, had lost part of its minefield. Through lack of maintenance, its surrounding anti-tank ditch had also become silted up.

At dawn on June 20, whilst the 90th Light Division and the "Littorio" Armoured Division, recently arrived in the battle area, covered the 8th Army, or what was left of it, Rommel attacked Tobruk with his two Panzer divisions and

the Italian XX Corps. The attack was from the south-east and was supported by Stukas. By 0800 hours the forward troops of the 15th Panzer Division had bridged the anti-tank ditch so that the armour could immediately exploit the breach, and by mid-day the ships at anchor in the harbour were being pounded by heavy artillery. The battle raged until nightfall around the Solaro and Pilastrino forts, where finally the 21st Panzer Division hoisted the Swastika flag.

In these desperate conditions, at 0940 hours on June 21, Major-General H. B. Klopper surrendered to General Navarrini the garrison of Tobruk, that is 33,000 men of the 2nd South African Division, the 11th Indian Brigade, the 32nd Army Tank Brigade, and the 201st Guards Brigade. A considerable number of vehicles and 2,200,000 gallons of petrol fell into Axis hands. A few hours later, Rommel, quot-

△ *The crew of a captured mortar watch from their pit to see where the bomb they have just fired will land.*

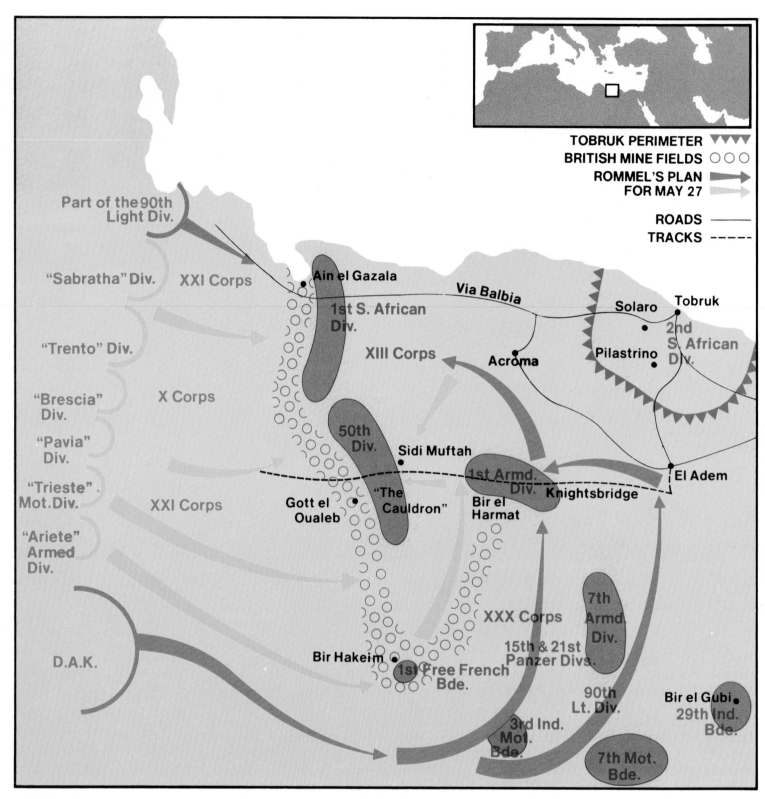

Map labels

TOBRUK PERIMETER ▼▼▼▼
BRITISH MINE FIELDS ○○○
ROMMEL'S PLAN ➤
FOR MAY 27 ➤
ROADS ───
TRACKS ─ ─ ─

Part of the 90th Light Div.

"Sabratha" Div.

XXI Corps

Ain el Gazala

Via Balbia

Solaro

Tobruk

"Trento" Div.

1st S. African Div.

XIII Corps

Acroma

Pilastrino

2nd S. African Div.

X Corps

"Brescia" Div.

"Pavia" Div.

50th Div.

Sidi Muftah

1st Armd. Div.

El Adem

"Trieste" Mot. Div.

XXI Corps

Gott el Oualeb

"The Cauldron"

Bir el Harmat

Knightsbridge

"Ariete" Armed Div.

7th Armd. Div.

XXX Corps

15th & 21st Panzer Divs.

D.A.K.

Bir Hakeim

1st Free French Bde.

90th Lt. Div.

Bir el Gubi

29th Ind. Bde.

3rd Ind. Mot. Bde.

7th Mot. Bde.

△ *The Battle of Gazala. The 8th Army was planning an offensive, but Rommel struck first, circling round the 8th Army's left wing and striking deep into its rear areas. However, the Free French held on at Bir Hakeim and Rommel, short of fuel and water, had to fall back. The British reacted slowly, and Rommel managed to save his forces, plunging on to take Tobruk. It now looked as though nothing could stop Rommel driving through to the Suez Canal.*

May 26: Rommel's Italian infantry under Crüwell launches frontal assault against Gazala Line at 1400 hours. At 2030 Rommel orders *"Venezia"* and the great wheeling movement of the Afrika Korps around Bir Hakeim gets under way.
May 27: Rommel's plan to overrun the 8th Army east of the Gazala Line fails. Afrika Korps suffers heavy losses; Bir Hakeim holds out.
May 28: Rommel begins to concentrate Afrika Korps, "Ariete", and 90th Light in the "Cauldron", planning a central breakthrough of the Gazala Line minefields and the reduction of Bir Hakeim before resuming his advance to the north.
May 29–June 9: attrition fighting in the "Cauldron"

and mass attacks on Bir Hakeim.
June 5–6: Piecemeal British tank counter-attacks are repulsed with heavy loss.
June 10: German forces break through the Gazala Line north of Bir Hakeim.
June 10–11: Bir Hakeim garrison breaks out during the night.
June 11–13: Fierce tank battles give Rommel armour superiority. The Guards evacuate Knightsbridge box.
June 14–16: 8th Army begins withdrawal. Troops pull back into Tobruk perimeter. Rommel takes El Adem, Belhamed and Sidi Rezegh; Tobruk is isolated.
June 17–20: Rommel regroups and attacks Tobruk.
June 21: Tobruk garrison surrenders.

ing the 45,000 prisoners taken since May 27, together with 1,000 armoured vehicles, and 400 guns, addressed a glowing order of the day to his men. He ended with this meaningful appeal:

"Soldiers of the *Panzerarmee Afrika*!

"Now for the complete destruction of the enemy. We will not rest until we have shattered the last remnants of the British 8th Army. During the days to come, I shall call on you for one more great effort to bring us this final goal."

And he designated Sidi Barrani as the next objective for his victorious troops.

The Axis problem: Malta or Suez?

It had, however, been agreed that the bulk of the *Panzerarmee* would not go beyond Halfaya Pass and that from June 20 some of its detachments would be withdrawn so that *Esigenza "C3"* or Operation *"Herkules"* could be started on August 1. Cavallero in Rome was still keeping to what had been agreed at Klessheim, and on the very day when Rommel announced his intention of disobeying his directive of May 5, he had the Duce sign a letter reminding Hitler of the great importance he attached to an early solution of the Malta question, asking the Duce to say in particular:

"This action against Malta is more imperative than ever. The truly remarkable effects of the mass action by the Axis air forces, and in particular of *Luftflotte* II in April, were still being felt in May. But in June Malta was being constantly re-supplied with planes and it has recovered its offensive powers so that now our sea-borne routes towards Libya are again under threat. As things stand, we must be able to conduct our transport operations with sufficient security if the results achieved in Marmarica are to be maintained and our future needs met."

Objective Suez

But at German headquarters Hitler had become much less enthusiastic over the Malta enterprise. In his reply dated June 23 he never even mentioned it. He urged his ally not to imitate the British, who in the previous year had gone off chasing shadows in Greece when they could have occupied Tripoli. And, moreover, there was the danger of U.S. heavy bombers based in Egypt attacking Italy. Finally the conquest of Egypt, combined with the effects of the campaign which had started with the attack on Sevastopol', would be the end of British rule in the Middle East. At this historic hour, which would not return, the Führer advised the Duce to order Rommel to pursue the enemy's forces to complete annihilation. "In war," he noted sententiously, "the goddess of Fortune visits captains only once. He who does not grasp her at such a moment will never reach her again."

Mussolini gave in to his ally's point of view and his Chief of General Staff had to agree. When Hitler was addressing this exhortation to his friend the Duce, Rommel, who had just been promoted Field-Marshal, had already driven beyond Sidi Barrani. And so in Derna, where Cavallero, accompanied by Kesselring and Weichold, had come to talk to him, the discussion was not about the alternative, Malta or Suez, but whether a pause was desirable ˙before the El Alamein gap or whether they should try to rush through it. Forgetting his saying "Tobruk – the Nile: it's only a dream", Cavallero finally gave in to the more ambitious solution of his German colleagues.

Auchinleck assumes personal control

At the same time the Panzers were approaching Marsa Matrûh, where Lieutenant-General Ritchie had awkwardly let himself get caught. Sir Claude Auchinleck then took over from Ritchie's hesitant hands the reins of the 8th Army. Both at the time and since, much has been said about Ritchie's responsibility for the defeats of January and June 1942. We will merely state that the last time he had led troops was in 1938, as the commander of an infantry battalion, and that he had therefore little experience of the tactical and technical considerations required in army operations. It should also be stated that when commanding a corps in the 1944–1945 campaign he satisfied so demanding and punctilious a leader as Field-Marshal Montgomery who, as we know, could easily be displeased.

△ *While the Germans took most of the burden of fighting upon themselves, the task of guarding British prisoners fell upon the Italian infantry.*

The American M3 Lee/Grant Mark I medium tank

Weight: 26¾ tons.
Crew: six.
Armament: one 75-mm gun with 46 rounds, one 37-mm gun with 178 rounds, and four .3-inch Browning machine guns with 9,200 rounds.
Armour: hull front 51-mm, sides and rear 38-mm, bottom 25-mm, top 13-mm; turret front, sides and rear 57-mm, and top 20-mm.
Engine: one Continental R-975 radial, 340-hp.
Speed: 26 mph.
Range: 120 miles.
Length: 18 feet 6 inches.
Width: 8 feet 11 inches.
Height: 10 feet 3 inches.

The British Infantry Tank Mark III Valentine I

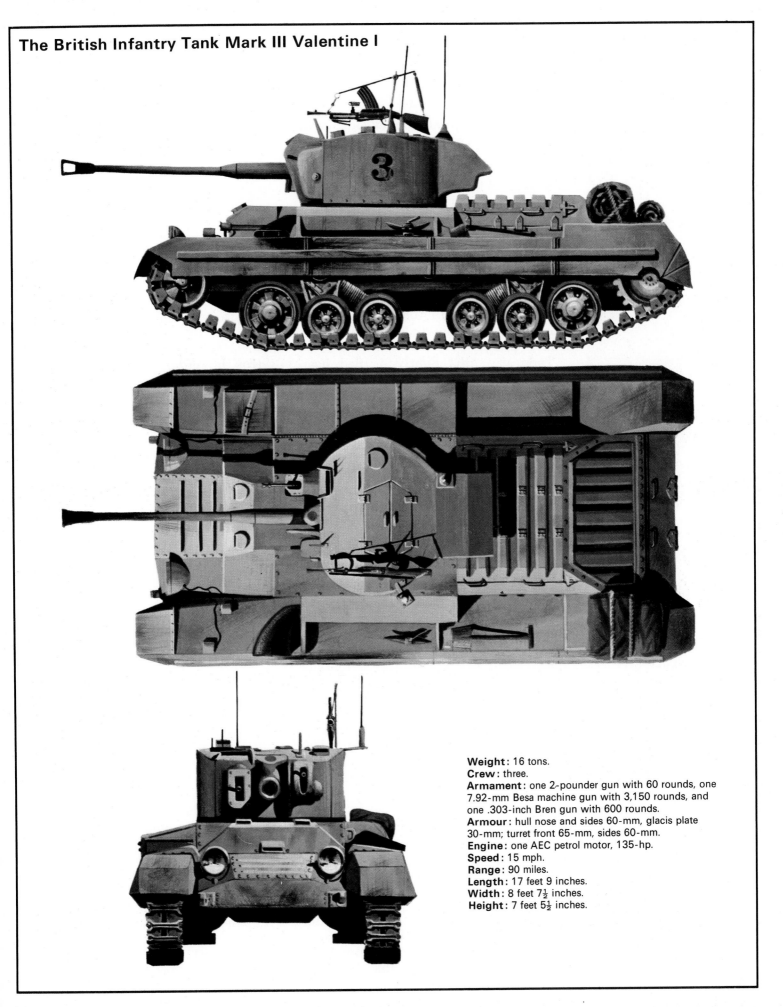

Weight: 16 tons.
Crew: three.
Armament: one 2-pounder gun with 60 rounds, one 7.92-mm Besa machine gun with 3,150 rounds, and one .303-inch Bren gun with 600 rounds.
Armour: hull nose and sides 60-mm, glacis plate 30-mm; turret front 65-mm, sides 60-mm.
Engine: one AEC petrol motor, 135-hp.
Speed: 15 mph.
Range: 90 miles.
Length: 17 feet 9 inches.
Width: 8 feet 7½ inches.
Height: 7 feet 5½ inches.

△ *General Sir Claude Auchinleck. On May 20 he had written to the 8th Army's commander, General Ritchie, giving his analysis of where Rommel might be expected to strike. There were two main possibilities: an out-flanking movement round the 8th Army's southern, desert flank, followed by a thrust towards Tobruk, or a narrow punch through the 8th Army's centre, expanding as it moved on Tobruk. Auchinleck himself thought the latter more likely. Rommel planned the former. Whatever happened, Auchinleck advised, the British armour should be used as a single, powerful force. His subordinates in 8th Army, however, had to plan for any eventuality, and the armour was distributed piecemeal.*

The 8th Army strengthens its position at El Alamein . . .

Auchinleck nevertheless managed to get X Corps (Lieutenant-General W. G. Holmes) out of the trap at Marsa Matrûh. This formation was newly arrived from Britain. It was not to be without loss, however, as the New Zealand Division, which took up the fighting again, was very hard pressed and its commander, Major-General Freyberg, was severely wounded. Even so, having a few days' start on the enemy, the remains of the 8th Army were able to take up position at El Alamein, where they were joined by the 9th Australian Division from Syria and the 4th Indian Division from Cyprus.

Tactically, this lightly-fortified position stood between the Mediterranean and the Qattara Depression, an area of salt marshes and quicksand impassable even to a loaded camel, which excluded any large-scale turning movement. Strategically, it left Rommel the difficult job of supplying his army over the 250 miles of desert behind him via a single road continually harassed by Air Vice-Marshal Coningham's fighter-bombers. One of these had already killed General Baldassare, commander of the Italian XX Corps.

The Axis advance had been so fast from Halfaya to El Alamein that on July 1 Rommel had only some 6,400 men, 41 tanks (14 of which were Italian), and 71 guns under his command to face the British position. Nevertheless he ordered an immediate attack. But all the dash of his 90th Light Division could not prevent this act of rashness from being crowned by failure. The following week he had 30 battalions under his command, but between them they had fewer than 5,000 infantrymen. On July 17 his four armoured divisions only had 58 German and Italian tanks between them.

. . . and counter-attacks

To put it bluntly, Rommel had overstretched himself. The British were constantly reinforcing their positions and beginning to launch minor probing attacks, principally against Italian units as these had fewer anti-tank weapons. And so it was that one after the other

the "Ariete" Armoured Division, and the "Sabratha", "Trento", and "Brescia" Divisions were severely trounced: on July 22 Auchinleck was able to report the capture of 7,000 prisoners in three weeks. In his notes Rommel uses hard words against his allies. According to him, for example, the "Ariete" "gave in" on July 3, whereas we know from official sources that when it did fall back it was reduced to the strength of one small company. What is certain is that the new Field-Marshal, who had invited Marshal Bastico to dine with him in Cairo on June 30 when they were at the Derna conference, had well and truly lost his optimism. On July 17 he wrote to his wife:

"Things are going downright badly for me at the moment, at any rate in the military sense. The enemy is using his superiority, especially in infantry, to destroy the Italian formations one by one, and the German formations are much too weak to stand alone. It's enough to make one weep". And the next day, the same story:

"Yesterday was a particularly hard and critical day. We pulled through again. But it can't go on like it for long, otherwise the front will crack. Militarily, this is the most difficult period I've ever been through. There's help in sight, of course, but whether we will live to see it is a question. You know what an incurable optimist I am. But there are situations where everything is dark. However, this period too, will pass."

Rommel envisages retreat

In this pessimistic view of things on July 23 he went so far as to envisage retreat, but Mussolini, Cavallero, and Bastico intervened and on the next day, having repulsed with losses a new attempt by Auchinleck to break through his front, he recovered his calm. The victor of Tobruk, in reporting that he was checked, blamed the haphazard supplies he got in North Africa during this decisive period from *Comando Supremo*. This complaint seems ill-founded for two reasons:

1. because in Rome the logistic services of *Comando Supremo* had calculated Rommel's requirements on the basis of the situation agreed with him in late March 1942 and confirmed by the directive of May 5, that is that the proposed offensive would have as its

The American Curtiss P-40D Kittyhawk I fighter-bomber

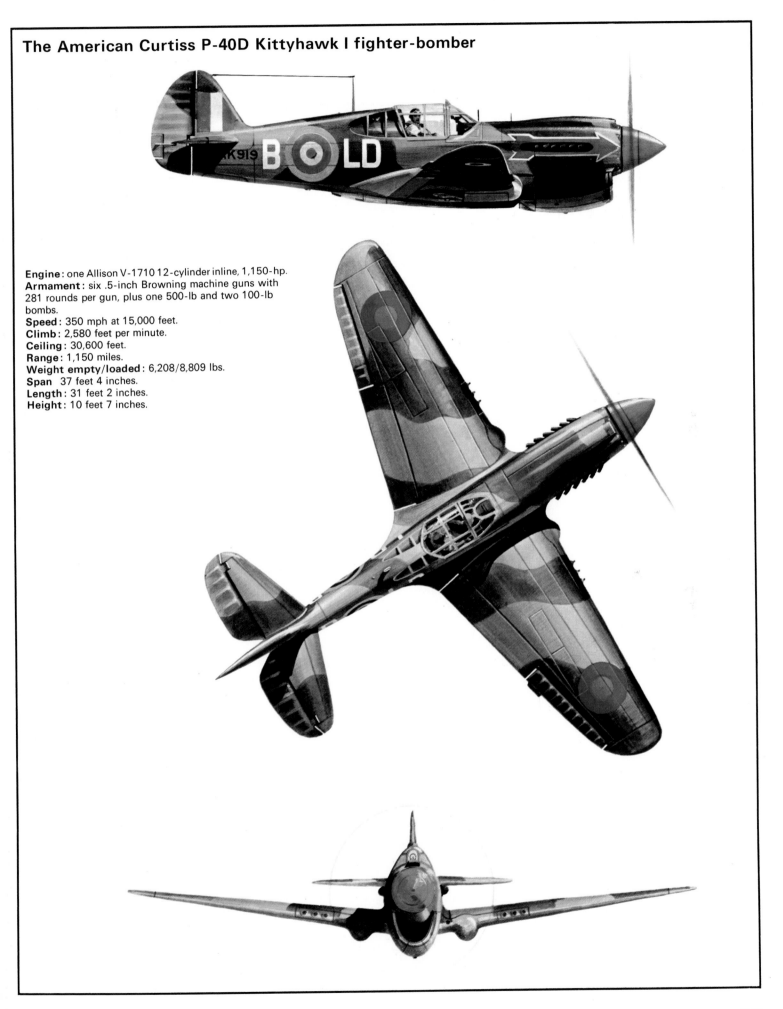

Engine: one Allison V-1710 12-cylinder inline, 1,150-hp.
Armament: six .5-inch Browning machine guns with 281 rounds per gun, plus one 500-lb and two 100-lb bombs.
Speed: 350 mph at 15,000 feet.
Climb: 2,580 feet per minute.
Ceiling: 30,600 feet.
Range: 1,150 miles.
Weight empty/loaded: 6,208/8,809 lbs.
Span 37 feet 4 inches.
Length: 31 feet 2 inches.
Height: 10 feet 7 inches.

△ The British destroyer Kipling *in action on a Malta run. While the Royal Navy struggled against the Axis naval and air forces to keep the sealanes to Malta open for supply ships and merchantmen, the Royal Air Force and submarines operating from beleaguered Malta struck back against the Axis sealanes across to North Africa.*

▽ An Italian freighter, crippled by an R.A.F. bomber.

objective Halfaya by June 20 at the latest; and

2. because the effort of improvisation demanded of *Comando Supremo* had coincided with renewed air activity from Malta. It was not Cavallero's fault if Hitler had transferred to the Eastern Front by mid-April a good half of the X *Fliegerkorps* and if several squadrons of the II *Fliegerkorps* had been kept in North Africa and Crete after June 20.

Britain's difficulties in supplying Malta

On April 25 Winston Churchill offered Lord Gort, then in command at Gibraltar, the job of Governor of Malta. Gort accepted the post, and all its burdens, without a moment's hesitation. When he arrived at Valletta he found the situation as follows: air attacks on the island's installations were decreasing, for reasons which we have seen, and this allowed the R.A.F. to send back there a small number of Wellingtons and Beaufort torpedo-carrying aircraft. But, because of the blockade, the population was reduced to ten ounces of bread a day and petrol was so scarce that contemporary photographs show us the new governor inspecting his command by bicycle. A new supply operation was all the more urgent because further Axis attacks were expected at any moment, and the defences could not be caught short of fuel and ammunition. The Admiralty therefore decided to send two convoys to Malta, one from Gibraltar and the other from Alexandria. This would cause the enemy to split his attack.

In the west, under the codename "Harpoon", a convoy of six merchant ships entered the Mediterranean during the night of June 11–12 escorted by the A.A. cruiser *Cairo* and nine destroyers. In support was Vice-Admiral A. T. B. Curteis with the battleship *Malaya*, the old aircraft-carriers *Eagle* and *Argus*, three light cruisers, and eight destroyers. The minelayer *Welshman* operated independently because of her greater speed.

On June 14, 250 Axis aircraft attacked the convoy. *Eagle* was able to launch only 20. But a Dutch merchant ship was lost and the cruiser *Liverpool* was so badly damaged that she had to be towed back to Gibraltar. As night fell, the supporting heavy ships turned back abreast of Bizerta and the convoy with its escort entered the Skerki Channel. At dawn on June 15 they ran into the Italian 7th Naval Division (Admiral A. da Zara) which *Supermarina* had very opportunely sent to patrol off Pantellaria. This Italian force consisted of the light cruisers *Eugenio di Savoia* and *Raimondo Montecuccoli,* together with five destroyers.

In spite of the Italian cruisers' superior fire-power, Captain C. C. Hardy, now the escort commander, turned to face the enemy and ordered the convoy to sail close to the Tunisian coast. During the ensuing battle the cruiser *Cairo* was slightly damaged but the destroyer *Bedouin*, totally disabled, was finally sunk by a torpedo-carrying aircraft. Again the British used smoke screens very effectively against the Italian ships, which had no radar, but they could not hide the convoy from the Axis aircraft which hurled themselves at their target. One merchant ship was sunk by bombs, while another and the American petrol-tanker *Kentucky* escaped the bombing only to be sunk by da Zara's guns.

Hardy reached Valletta during the night but he still had to reckon with Italian mines, which sank the Polish destroyer *Kujawiak* and caused such damage to the British merchant ship *Orari* that part of her cargo was lost. In all only 15,000 out of 43,000 tons of supplies reached Malta. *Welshman* acquitted herself well with her usual speed and discretion.

On the previous May 20 Admiral Harwood had succeeded Sir H. D. Pridham-Wippell as C.-in-C. Mediterranean. He was now given the task of directing Operation "Vigorous", designed to get through to Malta a convoy of 11 merchant ships with an escort of seven light cruisers, one A.A. cruiser, and 26

△ *Italian A.A. gunners wait for the inevitable appearance of R.A.F. bombers and torpedo planes.*

▽ *British destroyers move back into formation after breaking off an action.*

△ *British seapower–battleships to provide heavy gunfire, and aircraft-carriers to provide fighter cover over the fleet and strike aircraft against the Italian fleet and shipping.*

destroyers under Rear-Admiral Sir Philip Vian. But "Vigorous" was no luckier than Operation "Harpoon" in escaping the well-planned attentions of the enemy. On June 12 the Axis bombers scored a first point in forcing a merchant ship to drop out of the convoy and then finishing it off. On the 14th, after seven attacks by waves of 60 to 70 Junkers Ju 88's, a second merchant ship was sunk off Derna. Towards 2300 hours Vian learned the dramatic news that Admiral Iachino had left Taranto with his two 41,000-ton battleships and four cruisers, two of them heavy ones. At this news Vian turned about, calculating that on his present course contact would be established at dawn and, with 16 hours of daylight in front of him, there would be no escape. During this manoeuvre a German E-boat sank the destroyer *Hasty* and damaged the cruiser *Newcastle*.

In the headquarters which he shared with Admiral Harwood, Sir Arthur Tedder tried to hold off Iachino, unleashing against him all the aircraft at his command, notably eight four-engined B-24 Liberators manned by Americans and 40 torpedo-carrying aircraft. These relayed with the Malta-based aircraft which had been attacking since the previous night.

Vian made once more for the island. At dawn on the 15th the cruiser *Trento* was put out of action by a torpedo, but the Italians pressed on towards the convoy with three cruisers and four destroyers and the convoy had to take avoiding action for a second time.

At 1400 hours, however, *Supermarina* recalled Iachino, who now had no chance of engaging the enemy before nightfall. Informed of this by the air force, Harwood wanted Vian to make for Malta again. But Vian pointed out that he had already used up two-thirds of his A.A. ammunition and had to return to Alexandria.

Submarines and torpedo-carrying aircraft now harassed the retreating enemy. The British lost the A.A. cruiser *Hermione* and the destroyers *Nestor* and *Airedale*. On the other side, the *Trento* blew up after a hit from the submarine *Umbra* (Lieutenant-Commander Maydon), whilst the battleship *Littorio* was damaged, though not severely, by a torpedo from an aircraft. Malta thus got about 15 per cent of the supplies sent by the Admiralty. This undoubted success by the Axis powers had its reverse side, however: having used up 15,000 tons of diesel oil during three days of high speed operations, the Italian Navy was soon to be laid up through lack of fuel.

CHAPTER 66

Eastern Front 1942

△ Pzkw IV's of the 14th Panzer Division rumble towards the front through a Russian village. German tank production did not permit much numerical reinforcement of the Panzer divisions, but some progress had been made in giving them greater offensive power by fitting both the Pzkw III and IV with better guns. Armour was also improved, but crews still liked to carry extra track plates on the hull to provide additional protection.

◁ A German soldier questions some peasants, with a Russian prisoner acting as interpreter. Note that the German is carrying a Russian Tokarev rifle, probably taken from the prisoner.

△ *General Eduard Dietl, who commanded five German divisions, as the 20th Army, in Lappland.*

There have naturally been many books published, in French, German, English, Italian, and Russian, about the events on the Eastern Front between May 8 and November 1942. There are general accounts of the Soviet-German conflict; histories of particular episodes or army units; and biographies, or the "I was there" type of story, based on personal experiences. Finally, one must take into account the collections of documents from German military archives, painstakingly prepared for publication by the historians Hans-Adolf Jacobsen, Hans Dollinger, Andreas Hillgruber, Walter Hubatsch, and Helmut Huber.

Whose fault?

There is absolutely no question about the decisive nature of the defeat inflicted on the Wehrmacht by the Red Army on November 19, 1942. On November 5 Montgomery had smashed four German divisions at El Alamein. On November 23, no less than a whole army (five corps or 20 divisions) of the German forces were surrounded in the Stalingrad pocket. German and Soviet commentators do not dispute the importance and the consequences of these great events, but there are differences about their causes and those responsible for them.

All the German accounts concentrate almost exclusively on the evil genius of Adolf Hitler, but this is somewhat exaggerated. Most Russian publications assert that the German generals must also share the blame. This is borne out by a typical extract, written by Marshal A. I. Eremenko, who commanded near Stalingrad:

"The beaten Fascist generals may seek vainly to prove to their new masters, the American leaders, that they are not responsible for the failure of the Hitlerian adventure, and that it was all due to Hitler's mistaken directives, but they will not succeed. Can anyone fail to see that Hitler's directives, and all his strategy, were prepared by the German General Staff, those who are now criticising his plans? It is understandable that it is in the interest of the German generals to argue that the defeat was due to the wild caprices of a madman, rather than frankly admit the bankruptcy of their military doctrine, the superiority of Soviet generalship, and the stronger morale of the Soviet fighting man."

This is not a convincing argument. Since taking over O.K.H. (while still retaining control of O.K.W.), Hitler's interference in operations had become more and more extensive, and any objectors were silenced or ruthlessly eliminated. On July 15 he relieved Field-Marshal von Bock of command of Army Group "B"; and on September 9 Field-Marshal List suffered a similar disgrace. But the Führer, not content with dismissing List, then assumed personal command of the latter's Army Group "A", with the declared intention of leading it in the conquest of the Caucasian oilfields. Finally, on September 24, Colonel-General Halder was dismissed, since as head of O.K.H. he still refused to show the slightest enthusiasm for the Führer's intuitions.

On December 19, 1941, taking over supreme command, Hitler had declared: "Anyone can provide the limited command required for the conduct of operations. The task of the commander-in-chief is to create a National-Socialist Army. I know of no general capable of doing this, therefore I have decided to take command myself." On the day of General Halder's dismissal, he had also revealed his innermost thoughts: "The dictator complained bitterly of the constant and strong opposition he had encountered. He even quoted exact dates when this opposition had caused dramatic scenes and had deeply hurt him. This perpetual struggle had robbed him of much of his nervous energy. It was not worthwhile, however. To carry out the army's remaining tasks it was no longer a question of 'technical possibilities, but of National-Socialist ardour', which could not be expected of an officer of the old school. He even declared that 'the secret of Moltke's victories was to be found in his unshakable faith in the monarchy'."

Halder, however, almost as if replying in advance to Marshal Eremenko's accusations mentioned above, noted in his diary on July 23, 1942, apropos of a reverse in the Rostov sector destined to have important consequences:

"I have made known my express warnings, and now the results are only too apparent—we have fits of mad rage and violent accusations levelled at the commanders; his constant under-estimation of the enemy's capabilities is becoming increasingly absurd and dangerous; in short, the situation is more and more intolerable. It is no longer possible to talk seriously about our work. Unsound reactions based on fleeting impressions, with a total inability to assess the potential of his commanders–this is what he calls directing operations."

More divisions for the East

Just before the German summer offensive, the Third Reich's land forces amounted to 233 divisions of all kinds–that is, 25 more than when Operation "Barbarossa" was launched (according to Halder's table of June 16, 1942). Three of them had just completed their training in Germany, while 46 were on fronts of secondary importance–nine less than on June 22, 1941:

Norway and Denmark	12 instead of	8
West	26 ,,	38
Balkans	5 ,,	7
North Africa	3 ,,	2

It can be seen that naval forces were not the only ones affected by the Führer's "Norwegian complex", as it can be called, because Colonel-General von Falkenhorst, commanding in Norway, acquired a Panzer division. Moreover, Army Group "D" in Western Europe had to give up 15 divisions, but received the 6th, 7th, and 10th Panzer Divisions; Rundstedt took over command of Army Group "D" from Field-Marshal von Witzleben on March 15, 1942.

Operations on the Eastern Front were therefore carried out by 184 divisions: five of these formed the 20th Army in Lappland under Colonel-General Dietl, and were controlled by O.K.W., like units in other secondary theatres. O.K.H. authority covered the other 179 divisions in action between the Gulf of Finland and the Kerch' peninsula. These included:

122 infantry divisions
            (+18 compared with 1941)
3½ *Gebirgsjäger* divisions
            (+1½ compared with 1941)
6 light divisions
            (+2 compared with 1941)
19 Panzer divisions
            (unchanged)
11 motorised divisions
            (unchanged)
5½ S.S. motorised divisions
            (+1½ compared with 1941)
12 security divisions
            (+3 compared with 1941)

What stands out in the above table is the fact that the highly mobile Panzer and motorised units gained very few reinforcements. Those which benefited were the infantry and mountain troops, and also the security units–because of the increasing activity by Soviet partisans behind the German lines.

△ *The German six-barrelled 15-cm* Nebelwerfer *41 rocket launcher. It weighed 1,195 pounds, was fired electrically, and sent the rockets from its 51-inch barrels up to a range of 7,723 yards at the rate of six rounds every 90 seconds.*

▽ *A salvo of rockets lances out towards the enemy lines.*

Better equipment reaches the front

But if the *Panzerwaffe* did not benefit numerically, it did improve its *matériel* considerably. Not only had the production of light tanks been abandoned, but the medium and heavy vehicles were equipped with heavier armour and longer guns (5-cm of 60 calibres in the Pzkw III, and 7.5-cm of 43 calibres in the Pzkw IV). These weapons now fired armour-piercing shells at a muzzle velocity of 2,700 and 2,428 feet per second respectively. The 5-cm had the longer range. Of course these improvements meant more weight to be carried, but this did not affect the Panzers' tactical mobility. It is evident therefore that during the year the Germans had surmounted the crisis caused by the unexpected appearance of the Russian T-34.

At the same time, the increased number of tracked cross-country vehicles allowed the *Panzergrenadier* infantry to follow more closely behind the tanks. Thanks to their vehicles' light armour and cannon, the troops were able to do some of their fighting behind the tanks without leaving their vehicles.

Also, the Wehrmacht's Panzer and motorised divisions had begun to receive various infantry support weapons, anti-tank guns and even conventional artillery, fitted onto tracked chassis. For street fighting and assault on fortified positions they had a flame-throwing tank based on the Pzkw III with an 85-yard range. The little remote controlled "Goliath" tank, first used at Sevastopol', also had the same purpose. It was a wire-controlled tracked vehicle (modelled on the French Cloporte, produced experimentally at la Seyne in September 1939) capable of delivering a 180-pound explosive charge in front of an obstacle. The Panzers had thus made progress, but the other arms had not been standing still.

At this time the infantry acquired a new machine gun, the MG42, firing over 1,000 rounds a minute, and capable of repulsing massed infantry attacks on its own. The first rocket launching batteries also made their appearance, their official name being *Nebelwerfer* (smoke thrower). Before the war both the Russians and the Germans had made great efforts to produce rocket artillery. The Russians were ready first, having settled for a fairly primitive piece of equipment, the BM8 "*Katyusha*". These "Stalin organs", as the Germans called them, fired their first shots with great psychological effect on July 15, 1941. The Germans replied with a weapon consisting of six 15-cm barrels arranged hexagonally on a split-trail mounting. It fired salvoes of 80-pound rocket shells a distance of well over 7,000 yards, and those on the receiving end found them unpleasantly effective.

O.K.H. and O.K.W. worries

Whatever the improvements in its weapons, two questions caused concern in O.K.H. The first was over numbers of troops. On May 1, 1942 units on the Eastern Front were 308,000 men below strength. But it was calculated that men called up in 1942 would be arriving by August 1 to make up the losses expected in the summer campaign.

The second problem was that of keeping this increasingly mechanised and motorised army supplied with fuel. In spite of increased production of synthetic petroleum and supplies from Austrian, Hungarian, Rumanian, and Polish oilfields, the problem was becoming increasingly serious. On June 13 General E. Wagner, the Quartermaster General, head of the supply section of O.K.H., informed the Führer of his concern at the situation. In his view there was a great risk of supplies drying up by mid-September. Operations should therefore be limited according to supplies. "I couldn't expect any other answer from one of my generals," was Hitler's biting rejoinder. And yet Wagner had been optimistic rather than pessimistic, since from the end of July whole units were immobilised for days by lack of fuel. It is clear that Hitler's strategy found itself in a vicious circle: he needed oil to conquer the Caucasus, and at the same time he needed the Caucasus to obtain oil.

At a higher level, at O.K.W., another no less worrying problem was emerging. The development of R.A.F. Bomber Command, and the appearance over Holland on July 4 of the first American aircraft, forced Hitler and Göring to commit more and more forces to the defence of German ports and the Ruhr industrial basin. At the end of the year, three-quarters of German fighter strength were in the West. Fighter protection for bomber squadrons in the East was thus correspondingly

◁ ◁ ◁ *Rumanian troops march through Odessa. By November 1942, the Rumanian forces serving alongside the Germans totalled 25 divisions, formed into two armies.*
◁ ◁*Marshal Ion Antonescu, pro-German dictator of Rumania.*
▽ ◁ *Rumanian cavalry. Despite the increasingly mechanised aspect of the war, the vast distances of the Eastern Front meant that there was still an important rôle for cavalry, probing through gaps in the enemy line into the rear areas.*
△ *General Franco's contribution: Spanish troops of the* Azúl *Division.*

▽ *Italian gunners, part of General Gariboldi's 8th Army, prepare for combat.*

The Russian Ilyushin Il-2 "Shturmovik" ground attack aircraft

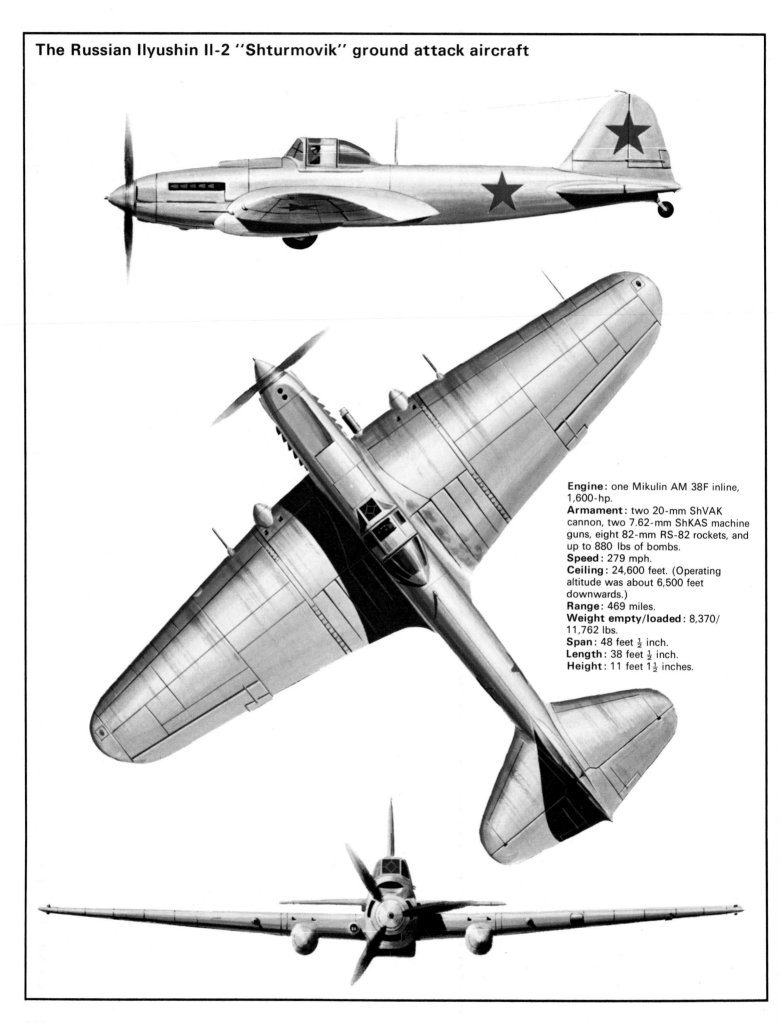

Engine: one Mikulin AM 38F inline, 1,600-hp.
Armament: two 20-mm ShVAK cannon, two 7.62-mm ShKAS machine guns, eight 82-mm RS-82 rockets, and up to 880 lbs of bombs.
Speed: 279 mph.
Ceiling: 24,600 feet. (Operating altitude was about 6,500 feet downwards.)
Range: 469 miles.
Weight empty/loaded: 8,370/11,762 lbs.
Span: 48 feet $\frac{1}{2}$ inch.
Length: 38 feet $\frac{1}{2}$ inch.
Height: 11 feet $1\frac{1}{2}$ inches.

weak, so it was more and more difficult for these bombers to play their part in the thick of land operations. In the autumn, faced with the Russian Air Force, continually reinforced by Lend-Lease deliveries, the Luftwaffe no longer enjoyed its numerical superiority of the year before.

The satellites' contribution

In the name of the "crusade against Bolshevism" that he had proclaimed on June 22, 1941, and of what he called the defence of "Europe", Hitler called upon all his allies and satellites to increase their contribution to the Russian campaign.

As a result of losses during the winter of 1939–1940, Finland could keep its 18 divisions in action only between the Arctic circle and the Karelian isthmus; General Franco did no more than maintain the *Azúl* Division in the Novgorod sector; and the Slovak contingent which took part in the Caucasus invasion was reinforced by a motorised division. Rome, Budapest, and Bucharest made a more positive response to the German appeal, as shown by the numbers of their troops on the Eastern Front in 1941 and 1942:

	November 15, 1941	November 15, 1942
Italy	3 divisions	10 divisions
Hungary	3 brigades	10 divisions
Rumania	15 divisions	25 divisions

Instead of the 52 satellite divisions and brigades fighting with the Germans from June 22, 1941, there were, just before Stalingrad, 65 allied divisions on the Eastern Front. Forty-six of these were wholly or partially involved in some way or another by the great catastrophe of November 19, 1942.

O.K.H. calculated that, given their differences in arms and equipment, three allied divisions were the equivalent of two German divisions. On this basis, the contribution of Hitler's allies in this phase of the campaign was the equivalent of 44 German divisions. And on July 1 Field-Marshal von Bock commanded in the Crimea and the Ukraine 29 such divisions, of which 12 were Rumanian, ten Hungarian, six Italian, and one Slovak.

These were Hitler's forces at the opening of the German summer offensive. They amounted in all to some 215 divisions (184 German, plus 46 satellite divisions, i.e. 31 in German equivalents)–35 more than on June 22, 1941.

Russian reorganisation

One would like to be able to give with the same precision the numbers of Red Army troops involved when operations again became possible. But even today, Russian historians maintain a peculiar silence on this subject. Of course from time to time we are given the order of battle and varying fortunes of some division which participated in a particular action during this second phase of the 'Great Patriotic War'. But there is not enough information to obtain an overall view. As for western historians' calculations, they are all based, in the end, on the situation tables prepared at intervals for his superiors by Colonel R. Gehlen, who had succeeded General E. Kinzel as head of "Section East" of O.K.H. Intelligence early in April 1942. These by no means settle all the uncertainties.

There is more information, however, about the structural reorganisations carried out by the Russians in the light of

△ A shot-down "Shturmovik". One of the greatest fighting aircraft ever designed, the Il-2 entered service in 1941 and soon gained a formidable reputation: to the Germans it was the Schwarz Tod *or* Black Death. *Immensely strong, and packing a very powerful offensive armament, the Il-2 was built up round a central "bath", comprising the whole forward fuselage, made of armour plate varying between 5 and 13 millimetres in thickness. This alone weighed something in the order of 1,540 pounds. Small arms fire was incapable of penetrating this, and as the aircraft was normally operated at very low altitude, A.A. guns had little chance of scoring a decisive hit. The Il-2's most vulnerable spot was the rear fuselage, and late in 1942 a new model, the Il-2m3 two-seater with a rear gunner armed with a 12.7-mm machine gun, appeared. This meant that the German fighters now had a far more formidable task when trying to shoot down this great close support aircraft.*

△ *Final inspection of a batch of Russian 120-mm mortars before despatch to the front. The Russians, perhaps more than any other combatant, were great believers in the efficiency of massed mortar barrages. Each Russian artillery division included a brigade of 108 120-mm mortars.*

▽ *The final assembly line for 203-mm howitzers on tracked chassis in the "Bolshevik" artillery works in Leningrad. The provision of tracked chassis for artillery proved very useful, giving the guns greater mobility.*

the preceding year's experience, which, in general, was correctly interpreted. The infantry division was reduced considerably in numbers. It now contained no more than about 10,000 men, that is almost half the number in a corresponding German division; and its organic heavy artillery regiment was also withdrawn. Thanks to the widespread use of individual automatic weapons, the infantry's firepower was still not significantly inferior to that of the Germans. In addition, their anti-tank weapons were increased, including 210 14.5-mm anti-tank rifles and 102 57-mm anti-tank guns. But to judge by the ease with which the Panzers broke through all resistance between May and July, it seems clear that these reinforcements were far from complete when Hitler launched his three attacks. Finally, the various services attached to the Russian division were reduced to an absolute minimum.

As for the armoured units, the independent tank brigades still existed. There were one or two of them in each army to use their weight and firepower in an infantry support rôle. The Russians were still, and would remain, attached to the tank support system in spite of its apparent failures during two years of Blitzkrieg operations. These brigades each had three battalions, 60 T-34's, with a squadron of T-70 light tanks for advanced reconnaissance work. As integral parts of each brigade there were also a battalion of motorised infantry, plus supply, maintenance, and repair services.

It was a 1942 innovation to group them in twos with a motorised infantry brigade to form tank corps, which were, in a sense, a Front (army group) commander's personal strike force. He would send them

in to widen and deepen breaches in enemy positions made by infantry units and their organic armour. But, as Moscow H.Q. repeated incessantly, such actions should avoid wild onslaughts and any engagements whatsoever with enemy tanks. Communications between armour, infantry, and artillery had to be maintained throughout the attack.

Transporting infantry was a difficulty for the Russians, as they had no tracked cross-country vehicles, but they got over the problem by carrying troops on tanks. The T-34 carried between 20 and 30, and therefore an armoured brigade could transport a whole battalion. In the same year the first self-propelled guns also made their appearance in the Red Army, though only in small numbers.

It has already been mentioned that the infantry divisions had to give up their 122-mm and 152-mm guns and howitzers. *Stavka* thus built up an enormous reserve of guns from which it would soon form its famous artillery divisions. Like the armoured, mechanised, and motorised corps, these were allocated to Front commanders as the need arose. It was also at this level of command that one found the brigades of *Katyushas*, as they were known to the Russian troops, rocket launchers with 24 or 36 ramps mounted on vehicles, with an electrical firing mechanism for their 35-pound projectiles. At the same time, anti-tank brigades were being formed. Between July 5 and 13, 1944 they were to prove themselves very potent indeed on the Kursk battlefield.

It must be emphasised that this is in no way a definitive account of the many aspects of Russian organisation, or of the numbers of Red Army troops involved. Russian sources are too imprecise. But

one cannot fail to be impressed by the scope and originality of the efforts made by the Soviet political, administrative, and military authorities.

Hitler's objectives . . .

"In Russia the winter campaign is coming to an end. Thanks to the extraordinary bravery and spirit of sacrifice displayed by our troops, the defensive battle on the Eastern Front is proving a most striking success for German arms." This was the statement that introduced Hitler's Directive No. 41, dated April 5, which set out the Wehrmacht's objectives for 1942 in the Eastern theatre of operations. Undoubtedly it was not far from the truth at that time. But he did not stop there, and his second paragraph contained an appraisal of the situation that was very wide of the mark. "The enemy have suffered enormous losses of men and *matériel*. In attempting to exploit their apparent initial successes, they have exhausted during this winter the mass of their reserves, which were intended for later operations."

It was on this basis that Hitler's directive was drawn up, giving not only the objectives of the summer offensive but even the lines on which it was to be conducted. This document occupies no less than five pages in Hubatsch's *Hitlers Weisungen für die Kriegsführung,* but need only be summarised here. Hitler set his armies the task of destroying the last remaining enemy forces and, as far as possible, of capturing the main sources of the raw materials on which their war economy depended. To this end, but without prejudice to a Leningrad offensive, all the available German and allied forces would be concentrated in the southern sector. Their mission was to annihilate the enemy on the Don, to conquer the Caucasian oil areas, and to capture the passes giving access to the southern slopes of the Caucasus mountains.

. . . and plans

The operation was to be divided into several phases. First, the left flank of Army Group "South" would move from Kursk on the Don to Voronezh and, moving down the river, close a pincer by meeting the 6th Army from Khar'kov

(second phase). In the third phase, Field-Marshal von Bock's right flank, now commanded by Field-Marshal List and renamed Army Group "A", would force the Donets in the Voroshilovgrad area and move up the Don through Rostov to meet the rest of Army Group "South", which in the interval would have become Army Group "B". This new pincer movement would close on Stalingrad, either taking the city or, at least, eliminating it as an industrial and communications centre.

Then Bock, with his right flank on the Volga and his left in contact with Army Group "Centre" in the Kursk area, would cover List's rear while the latter, reinforced by the 11th Army (after forcing the

win the war in the East for the Third Reich.

Was this grandiose plan feasible? Some deny it; but if it is to be given any credibility at all, one has to be convinced that Hitler would have carried it out seriously and methodically. This is just what he did not do. He repeatedly departed from his original plan by intervening personally, sometimes in fits of his well-known megalomania and other times in fits of weakness (less well-known), as a result perhaps of alternating states of euphoria and depression brought on by Dr. Morell's drugs.

Was the Führer aiming still higher? It has not gone unnoticed that in his letter to Mussolini on June 22 he used the attack on Sevastopol' as an argument to encourage his ally to exploit the Tobruk victory and push on into Egypt. Anyhow, his navy chiefs seem to have urged him to complete Rommel's expected success in the Middle East and East Africa as well as the victory in the East. Thus on June 12 Vice-Admiral K. Fricke, Chief of Naval Staff (Operations), and Captain Assmann put such a plan to the meticulous Halder, who was unimpressed and noted in his diary: "These people are dreamers on a continental scale. On the basis of their experience of the army so far, they readily admit that it depends on our enthusiasm and effort whether the Persian Gulf is to be reached overland through the Caucasus, or the Suez Canal from Cyrenaica

Kerch' Strait) pressed forward to invade the Caucasus. With this aim, the Rumanians, Italians, and Hungarians would position themselves on the Don between the bend at Kalach and the Voronezh area, while the German 2nd and 6th Armies, on the flanks, would be moved to the sectors where the defence would have no river obstacle to help them. This would be the fourth and final phase of the summer campaign that was intended to through Egypt. They talk of land operations through Italian Africa (Abyssinia), aiming for the East African coast.'' After having received his guests for dinner, he concluded with this somewhat sarcastic remark: ''much ado about nothing''.

Manstein settles the Crimean problem

However, before launching Operation "*Blau*", the codename for Army Group "South"'s general offensive, Directive No. 41 required Bock to take the last remaining positions in the Crimea and to wipe out the irksome Izyum salient, carved into the German lines on the right bank of the Donets and during the Soviet winter offensive.

At dawn on May 8 the German 11th Army, by substituting as many Rumanian troops as possible for German ones in LIV Corps besieging Sevastopol', moved over the Kamenskoye isthmus to attack the positions covering Kerch' with nine divisions, including three Rumanian and the newly formed 22nd Panzer Division, against the Russians' 17 divisions and three brigades, with two cavalry divisions and four armoured brigades. But if the Russians had a numerical advantage, the German 11th Army enjoyed superiority in the air, having Colonel-General Löhr's *Luftflotte* IV, including VIII *Fliegerkorps*.

Only Sevastopol' left

On the evening of May 8, XXX Corps had made an opening in the Soviet 44th Army's line (Lieutenant-General S. I. Chernyak). The next day its 50th, 28th *Gebirgsjäger*, and 22nd Panzer Divisions gained enough ground eastwards to turn north and drive eight Russian divisions back to the Sea of Azov on May 11; on May 16 a pursuit force reached Kerch'. On May 20 the remnants of the Caucasus Front retreated across the strait linking the Black Sea and the Sea of Azov, leaving behind them 170,000 prisoners, 1,138 guns, and 258 tanks.

Not wishing to belittle his victory, Manstein describes his enemy in his memoirs in much more moderate terms than does the *Great Patriotic War*, which vigorously criticises their bad position-

ing, inertia, and lack of communication, at the critical moment, between air and land forces. It reads: "The bureaucratic spirit which dominated the conduct of the campaign had disastrous consequences. The troops received orders which had absolutely no bearing on the real situation at the front. At the critical moment, instead of energetically leading their troops, the front commander, Lieutenant-General Koslov, and Army Commissar 1st class L. Z. Mekhlis wasted precious time in long and inconclusive councils of war." Consequently Mekhlis, who was also Vice-Commissar for Defence, was replaced and demoted, against which no one in the Red Army protested, for this man had taken an active part in the 1937 and 1938 purges. Lieutenant-General B. T. Koslov was dismissed, as were Generals S. I. Chernyak, K. S. Kolganov, and J. M. Nikolayenko, who commanded, respectively, the 44th Army, the 47th Army, and the air force on the Caucasus Front.

▽ *Ready for the offensive: German infantry prepare for what Hitler thought would be the decisive campaign of the war. In the foreground is an N.C.O. of a Panzer division doing a forward reconnaissance with the infantry.*

In his H.Q. at Poltava, Bock had chosen May 18 for Operation *"Fridericus I"*, a pincer movement intended to take the Izyum salient as ordered. But at dawn on May 12 he learned that his 6th Army (General Paulus) was itself being heavily attacked around Khar'kov. A few hours later it became clear that it was not simply a local attack but a major strategic offensive employing dozens of divisions and hundreds of tanks.

At the end of the winter, Stalin and his advisers in Moscow had refused to accept that they should remain on the defensive when spring came. On the contrary, they intended to attack. The *Great Patriotic War* includes this justifiable comment on their decision: "The Supreme Command G.H.Q. exaggerated the success of the counter-attack and ordered a general offensive in all important sectors, thus scattering their reserves."

Anyhow, at the end of March, *Stavka* rejected, because of lack of reserves, a plan put forward by Marshal Timoshenko which would have brought Russian forces back to the Dniepr between Gomel' and Cherkassy, and between Cherkassy and Nikolayev on the right bank of the river. Instead, they placed the South and South-West Fronts under his command, and gave him the much more modest objective of Khar'kov.

Khruschev is sent to Stalin

Timoshenko divided his forces into two. North, in the Volchansk area, the 28th Army (Lieutenant-General D. I. Ryabyshev) reinforced to 16 infantry and three cavalry divisions, and six armoured brigades, was to break through the German front and exploit its success towards the south-west. In the south, the 6th Army (Lieutenant-General A. M. Gorodnyansky: 11 infantry and six cavalry divisions, and 13 tank brigades) would break out of the Izyum salient, attack south of Khar'kov, and having broken through, then converge on the north-west, moving in front of Ryabyshev. Finally, cavalry and armoured forces would advance quickly on Dniepropetrovsk.

In the Volchansk sector, the 28th Army's attack, launched on May 9, was checked after having pushed out a salient of some 20 miles into the enemy lines. In the south, on the other hand, Gorodnyansky set General Paulus and Field-Marshal

von Bock a very worrying problem. On May 14 VIII Corps was nearly in ruins; on May 16 the Russians arrived at Merefa and Karlovka on the heels of the 454th Security Division, which had given ground, and a Hungarian division which had done no better. Sixty-four guns had also been lost.

In these circumstances, could Operation *"Fridericus"* retrieve the situation? Paulus and Bock doubted it very much, and on May 14 the latter noted in his diary: "Although I am most unwilling to do this, I can only propose, as far as the Army Group is concerned, to grab from Kleist [right prong of the *"Fridericus"* pincer] everything we can get hold of, say three or four divisions, one of them

armoured, and transport them to XI Panzer Corps' left flank. From there they will attack the southern flank of the enemy pocket."

In agreement for once, Hitler and Halder were intractable. Colonel-General von Kleist managed to save a day on his timetable and counter-attack at dawn on May 17. He fell on the Russian 9th and 57th Armies (South Front) under Major-General F. M. Kharitonov and Lieutenant-General K. P. Podlas, who had to protect the offensive by the South-West Front from surprise attacks. It is true that Kharitonov had only four divisions to hold a 65-mile front and that *Luftflotte* IV was applying its usual great pressure.

It took no miracle therefore for *Gruppe* von Kleist, with 15 divisions, including four Rumanian, to reach the Donets within 48 hours. Faced with this unex-

◁ *Dangerous cover. German infantry advance through a field of grain and sunflowers. The nearer man is carrying an MG 34 general purpose machine gun, and the other an MP 40 sub-machine gun.*

△ *The* Führerhauptquartier *meeting of June 1, 1942 at Poltava. From left to right those present are Hitler, talking to General von Salmuth, Field-Marshal Keitel talking to General Paulus, and with their backs to the camera General von Sodenstern and General von Mackensen (with Colonel-General von Kleist obscured). Also present were General Schmundt, Colonel-General von Weichs, and Colonel-General Löhr of the Luftwaffe.*

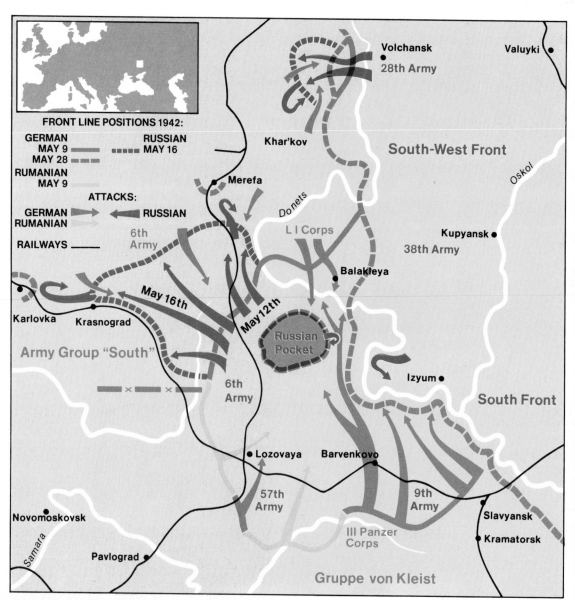

Volchansk
Valuyki
28th Army

Khar'kov

South-West Front

Oskol

Merefa

Donets

L I Corps

Kupyansk

38th Army

6th
Army

Balakleya

May 16th

Karlovka   Krasnograd

May12th

Russian
Pocket

Army Group "South"

Izyum

South Front

6th
Army

Lozovaya   Barvenkovo

9th
Army

Slavyansk

Novomoskovsk

57th
Army

III Panzer
Corps

Kramatorsk

Samara

Pavlograd

Gruppe von Kleist

▷ *The Battle of Khar'kov. The German forces, while preparing their own major offensive, had been surprised by the Russian attack, but had responded with considerable speed and assurance to turn surprise into victory, with a total bag of 214,000 prisoners.*
▽ *French infantry of the* Wehrmacht *move up through the ruins of yet another devasted Russian town.*
▷ ▷ *The bag: Russian prisoners taken in this first stage of the 1942 summer campaign.*

pected reversal, Timoshenko asked the Supreme Command to authorise the abandonment of the Khar'kov attack. This was refused, so he appealed to Stalin through N. S. Khruschev, political member of the council of South-West Front. During the 20th Congress of the Communist Party of the Soviet Union in February 1956, Khruschev explained this fruitless attempt.

"Against all good sense Stalin rejected our proposal and ordered that the Khar'kov operation must continue; and yet several of our army units were already threatened with encirclement and extermination . . . I telephoned the Chief-of-Staff, Vasilevsky, and begged him to explain the situation to Comrade Stalin. But Vasilevsky replied that Comrade Stalin wanted to hear no more about it. So I telephoned Stalin at his villa. It was Malenkov who replied. I said I wanted to speak to Stalin personally. Stalin's answer was that I could speak to Malenkov. Again I asked for Stalin himself. But he

continued to refuse, though he was only a few steps from the telephone. After having 'listened', so to speak, to our request Stalin ordered: 'Leave things as they are.' And what was the result? The worst one could expect – our armies were surrounded by the Germans and we lost hundreds of thousands of men."

Two armies destroyed

Khruschev's account may be somewhat embroidered but there is no doubt about Stalin's *"niet"*, and the results were disastrous. Unleashed at its appointed place, III Panzer Corps (General A. von Mackensen) moved up the right bank of the Donets, thrusting vigorously into the Russians' rear, and sealed off the Izyum bridgehead. On May 23 in the Balak-

▽ *Advance to the Donets: German troops take a quick rest before the final drive to this major objective. Shortly after his armies had reached the river, however, Hitler altered his plans and diverted the advance from Stalingrad to the Caucasus. It was to prove a fatal change of plan.*

leya area it joined up with LI Corps (General von Seydlitz-Kurzbach), thrown in by Paulus to meet it from the south-east of Khar'kov. Caught in the trap, the Russian 6th and 57th Armies counter-attacked furiously towards Izyum in the hope of breaking free. But in vain, for on May 28 the German 6th Army crushed the last centres of enemy resistance. Twenty infantry and seven cavalry divisions, and 13 armoured brigades had been wiped out, losing 214,000 prisoners, 1,246 tanks, and 2,026 guns. General Gorodnyansky was killed while fighting in the front line, and his colleague Podlas committed suicide with all his staff to escape captivity. Army Group "South" losses at this time were no more than 20,000, according to Field-Marshal von Bock.

While Stalin was still alive, Soviet historians did their best to conceal this major disaster. Since the sensational declarations by Khruschev at the Kiev Congress, there has been less reticence about its causes and consequences. In fact, on a throw of the dice, Stalin had wasted his strategic striking force, and before he could rebuild it Paulus reached the Volga and Kleist was threatening Groznyy. The military historian V. P. Morosov, explaining Timoshenko's position just before Operation "*Blau*", writes: "The reserves of the South-West Front were insignificant, since most of them had been used in previous battles in the Khar'kov sector."

The fall of Sevastopol'

The striking victory at Kerch' had freed the German 11th Army from any pressure on its rear, so Manstein was able to start the attack on Sevastopol' on June 7. He had received very strong reinforcements: three assault gun units, 24 *Nebelwerfer* rocket-launching batteries, and most of the siege artillery in general reserve. Amongst the last were two 60-cm *Karl* mortars and the 80-cm super-heavy *Gustav* railway gun, which fired seven-ton shells at the rate of three an hour. This monster's barrel was 100 feet long and weighed 130 tons. In addition, the Luftwaffe had provided 600 aircraft, including General von Richthofen's Stukas.

It was, nevertheless, a hard nut to crack. Commanded by General I. E. Petrov, the Sevastopol' garrison had seven divisions, plus one unmounted cavalry division and Vice-Admiral F. S. Oktyabrsky's three brigades of marines. It depended on 3,600 permanent or temporary fortified positions set up in depth over some 15 miles. Amongst these was the Maxim Gorky fort, with four 305-mm guns in two turrets. The Russians had no opposition for the enemy's overwhelming air power, however.

Manstein's attack involved three corps, including the Rumanian mountain corps, in all nine divisions, including two Rumanian. LIV Corps had the main task, to attack on the northern front, while XXX Corps with stronger forces took the southern front. It has been calculated that the German artillery fired about 46,700 tons of shells, and that the Luftwaffe dropped 125,000 bombs during 25,000 sorties in one month. But for all that, the

△ *The battle for Sevastopol'. A poster for occupied France extols the power of the German armed forces, and in this instance with reason. Aided by such powerful artillery, Manstein was able to progress slowly but surely to the overwhelming of the celebrated fortress of Sevastopol'.*
◁ *Men of the Rumanian Mountain Corps. While they held the centre of the Axis front, the German LIV and XXX Corps to the north and south of them closed in remorselessly on the garrison commanded by General Petrov.*

defenders were not intimidated. Each attack had to be decided by close hand-to-hand combat. When German infantry and pioneers had overrun the portions of any particular fort above the ground, they had then to overcome resistance in the labyrinth of underground installations, with the risk of being blown up with the defenders. And with destroyers and submarines the Black Sea Fleet worked hard to reinforce and supply the garrison. But although the German 11th Army's progress was slow, it was still sure and relentless.

On June 27, LIV Corps reached the north side of North Bay, and during the night of June 28 and 29 got its 22nd Airborne Division across in motor assault craft. XXX Corps had taken the dominating heights of Sapun. Sevastopol' was lost, but the defenders still gave the 11th Army a hard task. On July 4 Hitler had made Colonel-General von Manstein a Field-Marshal, but he had to wait until July 9 before the last stubborn resistance in the Khersonesskiy peninsula was overcome, fighting to the last cartridge and the last drop of water.

The Germans lost 24,111 killed and wounded, but captured 95,000 prisoners and 467 guns. The Germans were now in possession of the whole Crimea except the southern mountains, where there were still partisans, and the 11th Army was now available for other tasks.

Meanwhile the German 6th Army, not satisfied with having overcome the Izyum and Volchansk bridgeheads, itself crossed the Donets to secure a good jumping off position on the Oskol, the left bank tributary of this important waterway. This part of *"Fridericus"* brought in 45,000 prisoners, 266 tanks, and 208 guns.

According to Halder's table, already referred to, Field-Marshal von Bock had on June 16, between the Kerch' Strait and the Kursk area, 73 divisions of all types, including nine Panzer, seven motorised (two of them *Waffen* S.S.), and 26 satellite divisions. If the *Great Patriotic War* is to be believed, Stalin drew no conclusions from this impressive concentration of forces. Thus we read: "The Soviet High Command of course thought it possible that the Wehrmacht might attack in the south. It considered however that the enemy would not make its main attack on Stalingrad and the Caucasus but, with its forces before Moscow, would try to outflank the centre groups of the Red Army and take Moscow and the central industrial area."

Hence, in this author's view, *Stavka's* mistaken decisions during the first part of the summer campaign. Priority was given to reinforcements for the Bryansk Front which, if broken, would have let the enemy through to Tula and the capital. There is no doubt that this is what happened. But according to Accoce's *La guerre a été gagnée en Suisse*, the Soviet agent Rudolf Rössler had, from Lucerne, transmitted the text of Directive No. 41 to his superiors in Moscow. This was on April 14, ten days after Hitler had signed it. On May 3

Colonel-General Halder wrote this note: "*Exchange Telegraph* in Moscow is sending out surprising reports about our intentions."

Also, on June 20, eight days before the attack, a Fieseler *Storch* crashed behind the Russian lines while on its way back to the 23rd Panzer Division H.Q. In the aircraft, Major Reichel had apparently been carrying completely detailed operations orders for XL Corps. One can conclude that Stalin had therefore received more than enough information about enemy intentions from his Intelligence, but that he had ignored their reports. Why? Perhaps he thought he was being deliberately misled by the enemy, and clung more than ever to the belief that Moscow was to be the main objective of the coming German offensive.

Breakthrough on the Don

On June 28 *Gruppe* von Weichs attacked on a 90-mile front with its left south of Orel and its right at Oboyan. Colonel-General von Weichs sent in his own 2nd Army, the 4th *Panzerarmee* (Colonel-General Hoth), and the Hungarian 2nd Army (Colonel-General Jany), in all 23 divisions, including three Panzer and two motorised.

Two days later it was the turn of

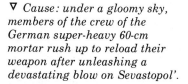

▽ *Cause: under a gloomy sky, members of the crew of the German super-heavy 60-cm mortar rush up to reload their weapon after unleashing a devastating blow on Sevastopol'.*

Paulus's 6th Army, which extended the attack another 50 miles, with 18 divisions, including two Panzer and one motorised. Paulus's XL Corps (3rd and 23rd Panzer Divisions and 29th Motorised Division) was to close the pincer with Hoth. It was a striking success. The left of the Bryansk Front (General Golikov) and the right of the South-West Front were broken. On July 1 the Panzers were at Stary-Oskol and reached Valuyki on July 3, while one of General Hoth's divisions stormed a bridge over the Don and pushed into Voronezh. This created a pocket in which 30,000 Russians were taken prisoner.

The Don-Donets corridor was therefore opened up according to the plan adopted on April 5. The Germans were to exploit this opening with Hoth and Paulus rolling through it to meet the 1st *Panzerarmee* (Colonel-General von Kleist), preparing to attack north-east across the Donets. Though fearing a counter-attack on his flank, Bock nevertheless kept his 4th *Panzerarmee* around Voronezh. This act of timidity cost him his command; on July 15 Colonel-General von Weichs took over Army Group "B", leaving his own 2nd Army, already in defensive positions on the Orel-Voronezh front, to General H. von Salmuth.

In spite of this error the 6th Army still moved on towards the great curve of the Don and threatened to overrun the South-West Front. This brought an order from Timoshenko on July 7 for a retreat. It meant that Army Group "A", attacking two days later, met only rearguards when crossing the Don. Field-Marshal List's forces, from left to right, were the 1st *Panzerarmee* (Kleist) and *Gruppe* Ruoff (17th Army and the Italian 8th Army) that is another 24 German, five Rumanian, three Italian, and one Slovak (including four Panzer and four motorised) divisions.

At the same time, Paulus was arriving at Rossosh' and a gigantic pincer movement was taking shape between Voronezh and Rostov, involving 52 divisions, including 18 armoured and motorised (about 2,300 tanks). On July 12 List extended his operation to the Sea of Azov, broke through the enemy lines at Krasnyy Luch, and five days later took Voroshilovgrad. This new setback, to say the least, forced Stalin to order Lieutenant-General R. Ya. Malinovsky, commander of South Front, to fall back in his turn. He perhaps intended to bar the enemy's way to the bend of the Don along a line from Voronezh to Rostov, but in this case he had not appre-

ciated the weakened state of his own forces and the offensive momentum of the Panzers.

So on July 15 Hoth and his *Panzerarmee* took Millerovo, having covered half the distance to Stalingrad in three weeks. In view of this situation, the next day Halder called together the heads of his Intelligence and Operations sections to discuss the possibility of lunging for Stalingrad without waiting for the fall of Rostov. He was thus remaining faithful to the spirit of the April 5 directive, while Hitler was moving further away from it.

△ *Effect: some Germans halt to survey the results of their handi-work from a reconnaissance vehicle.*

Fearing that the 1st Army might run into difficulties at Rostov, the Führer, from July 13, had placed Hoth, now reinforced by XL Corps, under Army Group "A"; then he had ordered it to swing from east to south-east. This brought it on July 17 to Tsimlyansk, upstream from the junction of the Donets and the Don, while Kleist himself had forced the Donets at Kamensk-Shakhtinskiy. Hitler remained deaf to the warnings from Halder and thought he was going to be able to pull off a massive encircling movement as successful as those at Kiev and Bryansk-Vyaz'ma, thus opening up the way to the Caucasus.

An enormous bottleneck and major supply difficulties then built up. But above all, without XL Corps' armoured and motorised strength, the 6th Army remained the only force still making for Stalingrad, instead of the two army groups as originally planned. Hoth's transfer prevented him from exploiting his newly-won bridgeheads on the southern Don and striking to the Volga. Paulus,

OPERATION "BLAU" ACCORDING TO
MAY 5 DIRECTIVE
STAGES   2
ACTUAL ATTACKS
FRONT LINES
GERMAN JUNE 28
NOVEMBER 18
ALLIED ARMIES
NOVEMBER 18

Army Group "Centre"

Lipetsk
Orel
2nd Army
Gruppe Weichs
Hung. 2nd Army
Kursk
4th Panzerarmee
Oboyan · Stary-Oskol
Voronezh
Hungarian 2nd Army

Army Group "B"
6th Army

Rumanian 3rd Army
Kletskaya
Italian 8th Army
Rossosh'
Don
6th Army
Rynok
Bazkovskaya
Stalingrad
Volga
Volchansk
Khar'kov
Valuyki
Kupyansk
Millerovo
Kalach
4th Panzer-armee
Rumanian 4th Army
Izyum
1st Panzerarmee
Voroshilovgrad
Kamensk
Verkhne Kumskiy
Kremenchug
Krasnyy-Luch
Don 4th Panzer-armee
Tsimlyansk
Elista
Dniepropetrovsk
Rostov

Army Group "A"   Gruppe Ruoff
Zaporozh'ye

Yeysk
Gruppe Ruoff
4
Kherson
1st Panzerarmee
Pyatigorsk
Kuma
Terek
Kerch'
Krasnodar
Kuban'
Armavir
Prokhladnyy
Groznyy
11th Army
Taman
Novorossiysk
Maykop
Nal'chik
Ordzhoni-kidze
Simferopol'
Tuapse
Sevastopol'
Black Sea
Sukhumi
Tbilisi (Tiflis)

▷ The advance towards Stalingrad and the fatal wheel towards the Caucasus. Whatever he did after this, Hitler was doomed – he had lost the only chance he had ever had, that of knocking out his giant adversary in one or two swift blows.

▽ Recruiting poster for the Red Navy. Deprived of a more active rôle at sea, the Red Navy units in the Baltic and Black Sea Fleets provided useful and able reinforcements for the orthodox land forces of the Red Army.

▽ ▷ The desperate struggle for Sevastopol', as seen by the Soviet artist Krivonogov.

ВПЕРЕД! НА ЗАПАД!

having to depend on his own resources, was forced to mark time while the enemy were using every means in their power to organise quickly a new Stalingrad Front.

Moreover, Paulus himself was far from overjoyed with the situation. Talking after the battle with his son Ernest Alexander, who had been wounded in a tank, he told him: "You can see the damage your tanks inflicted on the Russians. There are heaps of their tanks destroyed on the battlefield. We were told this story by a captured Russian officer – Timoshenko had been watching a tank battle from an observation post, and when he saw the rate at which his tanks were literally shot to pieces by their opponents he went pale and left, muttering 'It's frightful, frightful'." However, the wounded son sensed concern rather than satisfaction behind his father's spirited account of events. Paulus was certainly wondering what new reserves might be produced by the enemy who seemed, like Lerna's hydra, to sprout new heads as soon as the old ones were cut off.

On July 23 Rostov fell to Colonel-General von Kleist, but did not yield the expected amount of prisoners and booty. Hitherto in a state of depression, Hitler, again for no good reason, became once more optimistic. Hence his Directive No. 45, to carry out Operation *"Braunschweig"*. It was signed on July 23 at his new H.Q., set up at Vinnitsa in the western Ukraine to enable him to keep a closer watch on the current offensive. In his preamble he proclaimed: "In a three-week campaign the main objectives I had indicated behind the southern wing of the Eastern Front have been achieved. Only remnants of Timoshenko's armies have managed to escape encirclement and reach the south bank of the Don. It must be admitted that they will be reinforced from the Caucasus. The concentration of another group of armies is taking place near Stalingrad, where the enemy is likely to make a stubborn defence."

It was on these ill-conceived premises that he based the following orders for his army groups:

"A" was to:

1. occupy the east coast of the Black Sea from the Taman' peninsula, opposite Kerch', to Batumi, inclusively;
2. take the Maykop and Armavir heights, and by successive wheeling movements through the west Caucasian passes overcome enemy resistance in the coastal area; and
3. simultaneously launch a fast mobile force (1st and 4th *Panzerarmee*) towards Groznyy and then Baku. The Italian Alpine Corps would be used in this operation, blocking the central Caucasian passes.

"B" was to:

1. defend the Don between Voronezh and the great river bend at Kalach;
2. destroy the enemy forces concentrating at Stalingrad and take the town;
3. extend the line of defence between the bend of the Don and the Volga, up-

△ *July 4, 1942, and the German Army moves in to occupy its well-earned prize of Sevastopol'. Overleaf: German engineers take a breather as the first columns of infantry cross their partially completed bridge over one of the major river barriers so abundant in Russia.*

stream from Stalingrad; and

4. launch a fast mobile force towards Astrakhan' and block the Volga, downstream from Stalingrad.

The July 23 directive has since the war found no defenders on the German side. All the West German military historians' accounts consulted agree that the disaster which followed was the direct result of the decision imposed on the High Command by Hitler. To quote just one writer, the former chief-of-staff of LII Corps, Major-General Hans Doerr, who took part in the campaign with Army Group "A": "This July 23 must be considered as the day it became clear that the German Supreme Command abandoned standard principles of warfare to adopt peculiar new approaches stemming rather from Adolf Hitler's irrational and diabolical power than from methodical and realistic military practice. Once again history proved that Faith and the Devil triumphed over Reason. The trained soldiers around

Hitler were virtually impotent, under the spell of the Devil."

Of course Russian historians do not agree with Major-General Doerr's view. One can only quote here the opinion of Marshal A. I. Eremenko, former commander of the Stalingrad Front. He writes: "German generals will not succeed in proving that if Hitler had not forced them to get bogged down in the battle for Stalingrad they would have achieved victory and in any case would have taken the Caucasus in the autumn of 1942. The most important issue was not that Hitler was thrusting simultaneously towards both Stalingrad and the Caucasus, but that he had insufficient forces to fight both battles successfully. He had imposed this impossible task on his army to prove to satellites and potential allies the strength of the Wehrmacht (it was thus assumed that victory at Stalingrad and in the Caucasus would force Turkey, in the south, and Japan, in the Far East, to declare war on the U.S.S.R.)."

Eremenko's argument is not convincing. The "important issue" was quite simply that in ignoring the aim set down in Directive No. 41–first Stalingrad, then the Caucasus–Hitler ordered simultaneous and, what is worse, divergent attacks on the two objectives.

But this is not all, for the Führer made ruinous reductions in the army groups intended to complete Operation *"Braunschweig"*. In particular, the 9th and 11th Panzer Divisions were removed from the 2nd Army's inactive front and assigned to Field-Marshal von Kluge. An O.K.W. decision, dated July 9, ordered the S.S. *Leibstandarte* Motorised Division, which Hitler had not wanted to transfer, to France to repel any possible invasion landing. The excellent *Grossdeutschland* Division, held up at Rostov, would have joined them if it had not been sent on a futile errand to reinforce Army Group "Centre". Finally, though it had been planned that the whole 11th Army should cross the Kerch' Strait, it was decided that only XLII Corps and the 46th Division would take part in this movement, while six other divisions were dispersed to the four winds.

Eventually Army Groups "A" and "B", which had had 68 divisions on June 28, had no more than 57 on August 1. It is true that List and Weichs then had 36 satellite divisions instead of the initial 26, but it must be re-emphasised that these were not capable of taking the offensive. With

△ *After Sevastopol', Rostov, the key to the lower Don, became the German Army's chief objective and fell on July 23.*

▽ *One of the two German bridge-heads on the eastern bank of the Don. Note the amount of Russian* matériel *destroyed in the desperate struggle for this all-important crossing.*

reduced forces – besides the usual wastage from battle casualties – List and Weichs saw their two fronts lengthening inordinately before them:

500 miles on June 28;

750 miles on July 25, after reaching the Voronezh – Tsimlyansk – Rostov line; Over 2,500 miles, after reaching their final objectives, along the line Voronezh – Stalingrad – Astrakhan' – Baku – Tbilisi – Batumi – Kerch' Strait.

Even subtracting 1,100 miles of coast from the last figure, the remaining 1,400 miles suffice to show that the July 23 directive was the product of megalomania, of a sick mind.

But if Halder and his colleagues are to be similarly condemned, as Marshal Eremenko would have it, then surely Timoshenko and Khruschev must also share responsibility with their leader. For during the Khar'kov crisis they had passively obeyed Stalin's fatal pronouncement, transmitted by Malenkov: "Leave things as they are." But there is no reason to support such a judgement here.

Stalin's analysis

What would have happened if the Führer had stuck to the April 5 plans? Without going as far as saying that he would have taken Stalingrad in his stride, one can draw up the list of the opposing forces that clashed on July 22 at the great bend of the Don, between Kletskaya in the north and Verkhne-Kumskiy in the south, over a 130-mile front:

1. On the German side, six Panzer and three motorised divisions from the 4th *Panzerarmee* and the 6th Army, followed by the best German infantry divisions.

2. On the Russian side, the 61st and 62nd Armies of the Stalingrad Front, which, on July 12, came under the orders of Marshal Timoshenko on the South-West Front.

According to the *Great Patriotic War*, on July 22 the 62nd Army had six divisions in the line and the 64th only two; three more were moving up quickly by forced marches. But in the open plains 11 divisions extended over 130 miles could provide no more than an unsubstantial piecemeal defence. Also, the successive defeats sustained by the Red Army from the fall of Kerch' to the capture of Rostov had been a severe blow to morale, and a certain defeatism seemed to be gaining ground in its ranks. Soviet historians have been very discreet about this crisis, which reached its height about July 25. But it was serious enough for Stalin to issue his order of the day of July 28, of which the most important passages are

reproduced below, as published in A. M. Samsonov's work on the Stalingrad campaign. Summing up 13 months of war, Stalin wrote:

"Since the loss of the Ukraine, White Russia, the Baltic States, the Donets basin and other areas. our territory is decidedly smaller at present, and any reserves of men, grain, metal, and factories are much weaker. We have lost 70 million inhabitants and an annual production of 13 million tons of grain and 10 million tons of metal. We have now lost our superiority in reserves of manpower and cereals. To continue to retreat is to give up ourselves and our country for lost.

"Every inch of territory we concede strengthens the enemy and weakens the defence of our country. We must oppose pitilessly the view that we can retreat indefinitely because our country is rich and large, our population immense, and our grain always abundant. Such statements are untrue and harmful; they weaken us and strengthen the enemy, since if we do not stop the retreat we shall be left with no grain, fuel, metal, raw materials, workshops, factories, or railways. Therefore the moment has come to stop the retreat: not another step back! This must be our watchword. Every position and every yard of Soviet territory must be defended tenaciously and to the last drop of our blood. We must hang on to every piece of Soviet land, and defend it at all costs."

Stalin spoke of the satisfactory progress of Soviet war production and Hitler's mounting difficulties as he tried to achieve his objectives. He continued: "What do we need? Order and discipline in our companies, battalions, regiments, divisions, armoured units, and air force squadrons. This is our greatest weakness. If we want to defend and save our country we must impose much stricter discipline and order in the army. Cowards and panic-mongers will be executed on the spot. Henceforth every commander, soldier, and political officer must be subject to iron discipline. Not a step back unless ordered by the supreme commander!"

Perhaps Stalin wanted his subordinates to be blamed for the grim consequences of his own mistaken conduct of the operations. In any case, at the same time there was a whole series of changes and reshuffles of commands, both at front and at army level, which could indicate only a certain disarray amongst the generals.

△ An abandoned Russian A.A. gun, its barrel destroyed by the crew before they pulled back. Despite the number of excellent A.A. weapons available to it, the Red Army was still overwhelmed by the localised concentration of forces achieved by such formations as VIII Fliegerkorps.

The Germans approach Stalingrad

Whatever the weakness of the Soviet forces barring his way to Stalingrad, Field-Marshal von Weichs, as a result of the July 23 directive, had only the 6th Army to break through them. But even this was not complete since Paulus was waiting for the Italian 8th Army (General Gariboldi) to extend the line from the Hungarian 2nd Army (General Jany) on the Don, and meanwhile had to cover his flank with his own forces. Again, fuel was in short supply and he could not use all his armour at once. This explains his slow progress from the bridgehead he had taken on July 20 at Bokovskaya on the Chir. On July 30 Hitler returned the 4th *Panzerarmee* to Army Group "B", but Hoth, on receiving his new orders, was over 90 miles to the south-west of Tsimlyansk, and his orders were to move towards Stalingrad by the left bank of the Don.

On August 4 the 6th Army was nevertheless at Kalach at the top of the river bend, but the Russian 1st Tank Army (Major-General K. S. Moskalenko) got across the river and put up a stubborn resistance which lasted a week. Paulus finally overcame it with a pincer movement. His XIV Panzer Corps (General G. von Wietersheim) pushed from north to south to meet the XXIV Panzer Corps (General W. von Langermann und Erlenkamp) in the enemy's rear. A brilliant success, but the 6th Army was not able to exploit it until August 21.

On that day LI Corps, magnificently supported by *Luftflotte* IV and with insignificant casualties, established two bridgeheads on the eastern bank of the Don, upstream of Kalach. On the evening of August 23 the 16th Panzer Division, leading the XIV Panzer Corps, arrived at Rynok on the west bank of the Volga after a thrust of over 30 miles. Wietersheim was counter-attacked furiously from north

and south and wanted to retreat. Consequently he received the order to hand over his corps to Lieutenant-General Hube, commander of the 16th Panzer Division. A well-timed action by VIII Corps (General W. Heitz) relieved XIV Panzer Corps and made a defensive front possible between the Don and the Volga upstream from Stalingrad. LI Corps followed up its success towards the southeast, which allowed Paulus to combine his operations with Hoth's.

Making for the bend in the Volga by way of the left bank of the Don, Hoth had been reduced to six divisions, of which one was armoured and one motorised. It is not surprising therefore that with such slender resources he was stopped at the exit from Abganerovo on August 10. As Army Group "B" had no reserves it was up to Paulus to help them out, and he transferred his 297th Division and 24th Panzer Division. This was made possible by his success at Kalach. This reinforcement meant that the 4th *Panzerarmee* could renew the attack on Tinguta, but it was not enough for them to reach the heights overlooking the Volga downstream from Stalingrad. Failing further reinforcements, Hoth switched XLVIII Panzer Corps from his right to his left and pushed it due north. On September 2 he made contact with the 6th Army's right at Voroponvo.

The assault on Stalingrad

In his attack orders on August 19, Colonel-General Paulus assigned the objective of the south and centre of Stalingrad to LI Corps, and the northern districts to XIV Panzer Corps. The latter could spare only a fraction of its forces for this task because, with VIII Corps, it had to cover the 6th Army in the Volga-Don isthmus. It was not appreciated that this town, which then had 445,000 inhabitants, extended over 20 miles along the Volga and that, in places, there were five miles between the river banks and the western edge of the town.

This makeshift attack could only succeed if it met an enemy which was not only beaten but whose morale was extremely low. From the very first engagements in the streets of Stalingrad it was clear to the Germans that the Russians had recovered beyond anyone's expectations, and that the Russians' slogan "The Volga has only

▽ *A Russian infantryman waits in the ruins of a house for the Germans. Vicious street-fighting from such positions was becoming a vitally important part of the Russian campaign as the defence strove not to yield another inch of territory to the invader.*

one bank" was no empty boast. On September 16 Colonel-General von Richthofen, now commander of *Luftflotte* IV, complaining of the lack of spirit in the 6th Army, wrote in his diary: "With a little enthusiastic effort, the town should fall in two days." Less than a week later, he noted, more justly: "September 22. In the town itself progress is desperately slow. The 6th Army will never finish the job at this rate. Above all because it is threatened from the north by the Russians and because reinforcements arrive only in dribs and drabs. We have to fight endless engagements, taking one cellar after another in order to gain any ground at all."

At the same time, in the Caucasus, Army Group "A"'s offensive reached what Clausewitz called a falling-off point, beyond which wear and tear take over from the initial drive and energy.

The day after the fall of Rostov, Field-Marshal List's only worries were about supplies. It was impossible to satisfy the needs of 26 advancing divisions, some moving south-west, some south, and some south-east–so much so that Colonel-General von Kleist jested: "No Russians in front of us; no supplies behind us!" Jerricans of petrol dropped from Junkers Ju 52 transports had to be brought to the Panzers by camel transport.

In spite of these logistic difficulties *Gruppe* Ruoff (German 17th Army and Rumanian 3rd Army) occupied simultaneously on August 9 the port of Yeysk on the south bank of the Sea of Azov, Krasnodar on the Kuban', and Maykop (whose oil wells had been so thoroughly sabotaged that they were not in operation again until four years after the war). On the same day the 1st *Panzerarmee* took Pyatigorsk at the bottom of the first foothills of the Caucasus; on its left, the 16th Motorised Division positioned itself at Elista in the centre of the Kalmuk Steppe and sent out patrols towards Astrakhan'. On August 21 a combined detachment (to avoid jealousies) of the 1st and 4th *Gebirgsjäger* Divisions scaled Mount El'brus (over 17,000 feet), while at the end of the month Kleist crossed the Terek not far from Prokhladnyy, some 80 miles from the Groznyy oil wells.

It is true that the nearer they got to their respective objectives (Batumi and Baku), the more List's two groups became separated, and thus found themselves unable to co-ordinate their operations. In addition, Ruoff's outflanking movements over the mountains, intended to overcome resistance on the coast, became increasingly difficult as he moved south-east. On September 6 he succeeded in taking Novorossiysk, but he then had to reorganise his forces before tackling Tuapse.

Hitler reshuffles his commanders

Irritated by this lack of progress, Hitler blamed the local commanders. He therefore sent Colonel-General Jodl to Field-Marshal List to put matters right. But however loyal he was to his leader, Jodl knew his job, and when he was fully in the picture he approved the decisions taken by the Army Group "A"'s commander. On his return to Vinnitsa he made his report accordingly, but could not prevent the dismissal of List, who left his Krasnodar H.Q. on September 9. Moreover,

▽ *The foothills of the Caucasus almost within reach for the crew of this German 3.7-cm A.A. gun on a 5-ton ¾-tracked chassis. Hitler's premature diversion of troops to this southern lunge was to prove the undoing both of the attempt to take Stalingrad swiftly and of the drive to the oilfields of the Caucasus. From this time onwards, Germany lost the strategic initiative on the Eastern Front.*

923

△ *A shell bursts in front of a Pzkw IV advancing through a maize field in the approaches to the Caucasus (top) and the tank's accompanying infantry dive for cover (bottom).*

Hitler was so furious with the report that Jodl himself came very close to being ignominiously dismissed and replaced by Paulus. On September 24 Colonel-General Franz Halder had to hand over to General of Armoured Troops Kurt Zeitzler.

The new Chief-of-Staff of O.K.H. was said to be a National Socialist. Whether or not this was the case, it should be noted that, formerly chief-of-staff of the *Panzergruppe* von Kleist in 1940 and 1941, and then of the 1st *Panzerarmee*, he had only been appointed to this second post on March 15, 1942. On the same day he had moved to France with Field-Marshal von Rundstedt to become chief-of-staff of the latter's Army Group "D" at its headquarters in Saint Germain-en-Laye. He had thus been able to follow only from afar the disappointing progress of the second German summer offensive, and

was not in a position to appraise the causes of its undeniable breakdown. Hitler was therefore able to do just as he pleased with him, whereas Halder had for a long time kept out of his reach.

The Führer not only removed his Chief of General Staff; he also did not appoint a successor to List but proposed himself to direct operations on the Caucasus front. But all the genius and dynamism he credited himself with were unable to improve their progress. This was hardly surprising. Army Group "A" had had to reassign 4th *Panzerarmee* to Army Group "B" and had not received the promised 11th Army, and so was reduced to 20 divisions. Fifteen of these were exhausted German troops, there were only 300 tanks, and the campaigning season was rapidly drawing to an end on the slopes of the Caucasus . . .

Das Programm der britischen Plutokraten, ihrer amerikanischen Bundesgenossen und der jüdischen Drahtzieher:

① Polen mußte den Kriegsbrand entfachen.

② Norwegen sollte als Sprungbrett für einen Stoß in die ungeschützte Nordflanke des Reiches dienen.

③ Durch Holland und Belgien hindurch sollten die Franzosen und die übrigen Hilfsvölker Groß-

britanniens in das deutsche Industriegebiet und damit in das Herz des Deutschen Reiches eindringen.

④ Im Süden sollte Italien aus Nordafrika hinausgeschlagen und als »Gefangener des Mittelmeeres« als aktiver Bundesgenosse Deutschlands ausgeschaltet werden.

⑤ Die Balkanländer Griechenland und Jugoslawien waren als Aufmarschgebiete für eine Front im Südosten ausersehen.

⑥ Als letzter großer Vernichtungsschlag sollte dann schließlich die gigantische bolschewistische Dampfwalze über das deutsche Volk, alles zerstörend, hinwegbrausen.

Alle diese Pläne sind gescheitert! Jeder neue Versuch eines Angriffs endete mit einer neuen Niederlage für unsere Gegner.

Nach drei Jahren Krieg stehen die den Achsenmächten angeschlossenen jungen Nationen Europas geschlossen und siegreich gegen eine zusammenbrechende plutokratisch-bolschewistische Front.

Das neue Europa ist unschlagbar

CHAPTER 68
'Second Front Now!'

General Dwight D. Eisenhower was born in 1890 and entered West Point in 1911. In World War I he commanded a tank training centre, and after the war he was promoted to major. In 1926 he graduated first from the general staff school and in 1928 passed his course at the Army War College. From 1933 to 1939 Eisenhower served under General MacArthur in the United States and in the Philippines.

Eisenhower returned to the U.S. after the outbreak of war in Europe, and came to the notice of General Marshall during the 1941 Louisiana manoeuvres, after which he was promoted to brigadier-general. After Pearl Harbor he was moved to Washington to become Assistant Chief of the War Plans Division, in which he was responsible for preparing plans for the invasion of Europe. In this connection he visited London in April and May 1942 for discussions with British military leaders.

On June 25, 1942 he again arrived in London, this time as commander of the U.S. forces in the European theatre of operations. He commanded actual field operations for the first time in Operation "Torch". Supreme Allied Commander, North Africa, in 1943, he took command of the forces for "Overlord" early in 1944.

Although in the last 20 years Soviet historiography has made some progress in its treatment of military operations, the same cannot be said for it where inter-Allied relations are concerned. There, no advance at all has been made on the hostile attitude adopted in the Stalinist era – an attitude which we notice whenever it touches on the help given to Moscow by London and Washington in assisting the Red Army's fluctuating struggle against the German invaders. No one will deny that when it came to supplying equipment and *matériel* and to opening a second front, the two Anglo-Saxon powers were able to do little for their Soviet ally. But could they really have done any more in view of the other aspects of their strategic situation, which could not but occupy their attention? And can it really be correct to see a sinister plot secretly hatched out between the London and Washington Governments in this quite relative and temporary lack of assistance?

Soviet views on the Second Front

The second volume of *The Great Patriotic War* makes no bones about giving an affirmative answer to the second of our two questions.

But while its official nature constrains the satellite countries and the Communist parties of Western Europe to accept the thesis as an article of faith affirmed by Moscow, it need carry no weight with impartial historians such as ourselves. And if we apply to it standard tests of historical exactitude we see that it crumbles away and dissolves, leaving witness only to the extreme naïvety of those who, on this side of the Iron Curtain, believe it.

Dealing with the question of a second front, the *Great Patriotic War* quotes Eisenhower as saying that such a front should be delayed until German morale cracked. But the quotation only makes sense if it is put back into its proper context. What was Eisenhower talking about? Simply that "This was a very defi-

nite conviction, held by some of our experienced soldiers, sailors, and airmen, that the fortified coast of western Europe could not be successfully attacked. Already much was known of the tremendous effort the German was making to insure integrity of his Atlantic Wall."

Moreover, bearing in mind the capacity of the Luftwaffe, the strength of the Army, and the submarine and mine-laying potential of the German Navy, all of which would have been used to oppose an attempted landing, Eisenhower writes in his *Crusade in Europe*: "Many held that attack against this type of defence was madness, nothing but military suicide. Even among those who thought direct assault by land forces would eventually become necessary, the majority believed that definite signs of cracking German morale would have to appear before it would be practicable to attempt such an enterprise."

Admittedly, he says, General Marshall, who was Chief of General Staff, and Major-Generals J. T. MacNarney and Carl A. Spaatz (U.S. Army Air Force) were less pessimistic, but they were almost alone in their views. Be that as it may, it should be emphasised that the objections raised by the American military to establishing a second front in Western Europe in 1942 were based on technical and tactical considerations, and not on political ones.

The Great Patriotic War attempts to rebut this line of argument by appeal to the success of Operation "Torch": "The English and American Governments justified this delay by insisting that they did not have the men and the means to land on the French coast. That this piece of reasoning is senseless can be seen from the fact that the United States and Great Britain engaged considerable forces in North Africa in November 1942 and succeeded in landing both in Morocco and in Algeria."

A peculiar argument, we may reply, which quite ignores the serious military and political preparatory work carried out in North Africa by the American and English secret services as soon as a decision had been taken to land to the south of the Strait of Gibraltar.

As for the undertakings the London and

Page 925: *German propaganda map showing the strength of the "New Europe" and Axis plans for 1942, with an analysis of Allied plans up to and including the possible invasion of Italy.*
◁ *A Douglas A-20 attack bomber awaits shipment to Russia. Of the 7,479 built, Russia received no fewer than 3,600, more than either the R.A.F. or U.S.A.A.F.*
▽ *An American official checks a shipment of American-produced food destined for Russia's war-torn population.*

Washington Governments are supposed to have given Moscow, they were far less onerous than the Russians would today have us understand. Certainly, at the conclusion of the visit to the two Allied capitals made by Molotov, an agreed communiqué published on June 11, 1942 said:

"In the course of these discussions complete agreement was reached on the urgency of opening a second front in Europe during 1942."

But according to Winston Churchill, this declaration of intent was no more than a war-time ruse aimed at deterring the enemy from removing new divisions from the line between Angers and Cherbourg and transferring them to the Eastern Front. Should we believe him? Surely we should take into account the *aide-mémoire* he handed to Molotov when he left and which – to say the least – relieved him of any obligation as to a precise date for the planned joint operation. He says expressly:

"We are making preparations for a landing on the Continent in August or September 1942. As already explained, the main limiting factor to the size of the landing force is the availability of special landing-craft. Clearly however it would not further either the Russian cause or that of the Allies as a whole if, for the sake of action at any price, we embark on some operation which ended in disaster and gave the enemy an opportunity for glorification of our discomfiture. It is impossible to say in advance whether the situation will be such as to make this operation

▽ ▷ *American infantry in training in Northern Ireland during March 1942. Despite the gravity of the situation in the Pacific, the American high command was swift to send troops to Great Britain in preparation for the planned invasion of Europe. The 4,000-strong vanguard of this steadily growing commitment to the "Germany first" principle arrived in Belfast on January 25–26, 1942. Before crossing the Atlantic, American soldiers were given a 32-page booklet advising them on what to expect and how to behave in the British Isles. One piece of advice was "The British will welcome you as friends and allies, but remember that crossing an ocean does not automatically make you a hero. There are housewives in aprons and youngsters in knee pants in Britain who have lived through more high-explosives in air raids than many soldiers saw in first-class barrages in the last war."*

feasible when the time comes. *We can therefore give no promise in the matter*, but provided that it appears sound and sensible we shall not hesitate to put our plans into effect."

Molotov at the White House

At the White House on the preceding May 30, President Roosevelt had gone somewhat further. According to the account of the meeting given by Professor Samuel H. Cross, who acted as interpreter for the American delegation, Molotov had told his host:

"'If you postpone your decision you will have eventually to bear the brunt of the war, and if Hitler becomes the undisputed master of the Continent, next year will unquestionably be tougher than this one.'

"The President then put to General Marshall the query whether developments were clear enough so that we could say to Mr. Stalin that we are preparing a Second Front. 'Yes,' replied the General. The President then authorized Mr. Molotov to inform Mr. Stalin that we expected the formation of a Second Front this year."

Even though these words cannot be regarded as giving any explicit formal undertaking, it will scarcely enter anyone's head to suggest that President Roosevelt, advised by Harry Hopkins and General Marshall, would have offered his Russian partner deliberately false assurances. In the face of Churchill's determined opposition to any cross-Channel attack in 1942, Roosevelt had very reluctantly resigned himself to reviving Operation "Gymnast". But was he really in any position to ignore the resistance of his British ally when it came to an attack across the Cotentin peninsula?

Nevertheless, Hitler was still very worried about the possibility of a cross-channel attack. On July 9, less than a month after the publication of the communiqué quoted above, he despatched an identically-worded directive to Army, Navy, and Air Force, the first paragraph of which contained his assessment of the situation and deserves note.

"Our swift and massive victories may force Great Britain to choose between launching a large scale invasion, with a view to opening a second front, or seeing Russia eliminated as a military and political factor. Hence it is highly probable that we shall soon face an enemy landing within the O.K.H. command area."

In danger, he thought, were:
"(a) In the first place the Pas de Calais, the sector between Dieppe and Le Havre, and Normandy, because these regions are within range of enemy guns and within reach of most of their transport vessels.
(b) Secondly, southern Holland and Brittany."

On August 8 following, Hitler touched on the same subject in a long letter to Mussolini, in which he expressed both his contempt for his adversary and his confidence in his own resources.

"I consider the second front quite insane, but since in democracies decisions are taken by majority and therefore tend to derive from human incomprehension, one must always be ready for the fools to carry the day and to try to establish a second front." However, as he went on to explain to the Duce, everything was already set up both in Norway and in the West to give the invader the warmest of receptions. On the Channel coast and the Strait of Dover, fortifications were progressing apace and included numerous gun batteries of all sizes.

Whatever is said on this subject in Moscow, Hitler was alive to the danger and remained alert. He even proposed to go in person to the Western Front in the event of a landing and to assume command of operations on the spot.

"Any captain who attacks a shore battery is a madman," said Nelson, and that great sailor paid highly for his knowledge, losing his right eye at Calvi (1795) and his right arm two years later at Santa Cruz de Tenerife.

△ *General Marshall and Molotov* (right) *drink a toast to their common victory. Despite constant Russian claims that the Western Allies were being deliberately slow in opening the second front and thus throwing the burden of the war onto the sturdy shoulders of the Russian fighting man, inter-Allied co-operation was to improve and finally defeat Nazi Germany.*

Hitler was always conscious of the fact that he could expect an Allied landing somewhere in Western Europe, and so devoted enormous quantities of labour, matériel, and first-class fighting units to the establishment of Festung Europa or Fortress Europe. Despite his constant intuition that Norway was the "zone of destiny", France was clearly the most likely place for an Allied landing from Great Britain – sea passages would be short, and the French Channel coast offered many excellent possibilities for landing beaches. Thus an impressive and massive system of fortifications was built along the likeliest spots, with pillboxes, batteries, strongpoints, and railway spurs for heavy rail guns.

△▷ German rail guns, heavy pieces which, it was hoped, would be able to inflict heavy losses on any invasion force while it was still far offshore.

◁ As usual, it would be the soldier on the ground, such as this machine gun crew on the north coast of France, who would have to bear the first shock of invasion.

British and American flags.

As these figures indicate, the Anglo-Saxon powers had committed themselves to an amphibious form of warfare which, with rare exceptions, such as the American Civil War, had not been practised since the Norman invasions of the 9th and 10th Centuries. But they did so at the cost of enormous industrial and economic efforts which for a long time to come left their mark in one way or another on the general development of war-time operations.

American strategy

That this was so gradually became obvious later on, but neither Major-General Dwight D. Eisenhower, recently appointed to strategic planning, nor General Marshall were aware of it when, on April 1, 1942, they presented a plan of war to President Roosevelt. These comprised three separate operations:

1. Operation "Bolero" was to be initiated immediately, ensuring that within the period of a year 30 American divisions, of which six were to be armoured, should be moved across the Atlantic. These troops were to be complemented with air power whose task it would be to offer effective tactical support as well as to play its part in the R.A.F.'s strategic offensive against the industrial base of the Third Reich.

2. Once this logistic operation was completed, Operation "Round-up" should be set in motion, starting on April 1, 1943. It would involve 30 American and 18 British divisions, of which three were to be armoured. A vanguard of six divisions, reinforced by parachute regiments, would land between Le Havre and Boulogne. Strengthened at the rate of 100,000 men a week, this Anglo-American offensive would have as its primary objective the capture of the line Deauville – Paris – Soissons – St. Quentin – Arras – Calais. Later on the line would be extended in the direction of Angers.

3. Finally, around September 15, 1943, Operation "Sledgehammer" would be launched, with the limited objective of taking Cherbourg and the Cotentin peninsula. But in his memorandum to President Roosevelt, General Marshall made the execution of this operation contingent on the following considerations:

"(1) *The Situation on the Russian Front Becomes Desperate*, i.e. the success of German arms becomes so complete as to

△ *Work in progress on a concrete emplacement on the Channel coast. The priority allocated to such work came increasingly higher as clear signs of the impending invasion were seen in 1943 and 1944.*
▷ *America, with all her forces fighting overseas, was extraordinarily dependent on sea communications, with mass-produced merchant shipping, carrying men and* matériel, *protected by warships and naval aircraft.*

The experience of the Great War seemed to offer striking confirmation of Nelson's views. In the Dardanelles, English and French battleships, among them the powerful *Queen Elizabeth*, firing her 15-inch guns for the first time, had not succeeded in silencing the Turkish batteries which blocked the strait. The Navy had therefore requested the Army's aid in their destruction. But the landing of April 25, 1915, had run into a succession of disappointments and disasters, and the troops who were put ashore were soon to discover how weak, to say the least, was the cover and support supplied by the Navy's firepower.

In the period between the wars, a few men in France and Great Britain still interested themselves in the problems posed by landing powerful forces away from a large port. To this end they envisaged the construction of motorised landing-craft fitted with drop-gates in the bows over which to land their troops.

In France, three vessels of this type had been built by May 10, 1940. On May 14 the Royal Navy's landing craft put General Béthouart's *légionnaires* and tanks ashore near Narvik, and a little later 11 of these vessels had taken part in the evacuation of Dunkirk. The experience gained from these small-scale operations was encouraging enough to prompt the British Admiralty to order 178 of these craft from English shipyards and another 136 from American sources. For since the Americans foresaw a war in the Pacific, their Navy too had been concerned with the problem of effective landings in strength.

On the day of "Overlord", taking together all the military theatres throughout the world, there were about 9,500 craft of all sizes and types under the

threaten the imminent collapse of Russian resistance unless the pressure is relieved by an attack from the west by British and American troops. In this case the attack should be considered as a sacrifice in the common good.

(2) *The German Situation in Western Europe Becomes Critically Weakened.*"

These plans were enthusiastically recommended by Defense Secretary Harry Stimson, always afire, despite his 72 years of age, and by Harry Hopkins, mindful as ever of Soviet interests. President Roosevelt too, without totally abandoning his old preference for a North African

enterprise, finally came round and sent Hopkins and General Marshall to lay the plan before the British War Cabinet and the Chiefs-of-Staff Committee. On April 4 they left Baltimore by plane and on the evening of the 8th they met Winston Churchill, General Brooke, Anthony Eden (the Foreign Secretary), and Clement Attlee (Deputy Prime Minister since February 18, 1942).

The first conversations that General Marshall had with his British colleagues were reassuring. As Winston Churchill wrote in this regard:

"We were all relieved by the evident strong American intention to intervene in Europe, and to give the main priority to the defeat of Hitler. This had always been the foundation of our strategic thought."

British preoccupations

As often happens, it was not clear at the time to the two parties that they were not speaking the same language. Nor was it clear that the difficulties between them would come to light as soon as active decisions had to be taken. More than their allies, the British were concerned with the total strategic situation throughout the world, and at a time when a powerful Japanese fleet was at large off the coast of Ceylon they thought it important not to relegate the defence of the Indies and the Middle East to second place, and certainly not to sacrifice it to the initiation of a second front, which the American plan now envisaged for spring 1943. Such was the tenor of Brooke's speech on behalf of the Chiefs-of-Staff Committee to a meeting with Roosevelt's representatives summoned by the British Prime Minister on April 14. Sir Hastings Ismay records him as saying:

"The Chiefs-of-Staff entirely agreed that Germany was the main enemy. At the same time it was essential to hold the Japanese and to ensure that there should be no junction between them and the Germans. If the Japanese obtained control of the Indian Ocean not only would the Middle East be gravely threatened, but we should lose the oil supplies from the Persian Gulf. The results of this would be that Germany would get all the oil she required, the southern route to Russia would be cut, Turkey would be isolated and defenceless, the Germans would obtain ready access to the Black Sea, and Germany and Japan would be able to interchange the goods of which they stood so much in need."

At the end of the meeting Churchill announced that the overall plan could be unanimously accepted and that the two Anglo-Saxon powers, as brothers in arms, would nobly march together in the attainment of their common aim, a final victory. The next day Hopkins wired the White House that London had agreed to the essentials of the American plan.

As a matter of fact, only Operation "Bolero" had met with the full agreement of the British War Cabinet and the Chiefs-of-Staff Committee.

As expounded to him by General Marshall, the "Round-up" project did not appeal to Brooke in the least. In his diary he writes:

"But, and this is a very large 'but', his plan does not go beyond just landing on the far coast. Whether we are to play *baccarat* or *chemin de fer* at Le Touquet... is not stipulated. I asked him this afternoon – Do we go west, south or east after landing? He had not begun to think of it."

Maybe General Brooke was exaggerating a little. Nonetheless, "Round-up" certainly looked a rather ill-conceived idea. For landing between Le Havre and Boulogne, at the start of operations the British and Americans would have been confronted by natural obstacles serious enough to make the defensive bluff that overlooked Omaha Beach look like a trivial inconvenience of terrain. The German 15th Army, entrusted with the defence of the area, had received favoured treatment with regard to its equipment and could rely on more solid fortifications than were to be found anywhere else – not to speak of the enormous gun batteries which pounded the English coast between the North Foreland and Dungeness.

Besides, the best proof that this plan met heavy criticism is that it was abandoned and never heard of again.

As for the projected attack on Cherbourg, it was no more warmly received by Winston Churchill than by General Brooke. But while the British had time to wait and see before finally abandoning "Round-up", if they were to block "Sledgehammer" they would have to act quickly, for that plan was due to be set in motion on September 15.

Nonetheless, in this connection Winston Churchill was careful to avoid saying anything that might upset Roosevelt. So he offered no overt resistance, and was content to let the facts speak for themselves. Thus he wrote:

"But I had little doubt myself that study of details – landing-craft and all that – and also reflection on the main strategy of the war, would rule out 'Sledgehammer'. In the upshot no military authority – Army, Navy, or Air – on either side of the Atlantic was found capable of preparing such a plan, or, so far as I was informed, ready to take the responsibility for executing it. United wishes and goodwill cannot overcome brute facts."

Was the British Prime Minister guilty of overstating his case in order to discourage the White House? Not if it is true that, taking together all the landing equipment available at any one time in Great Britain, it would have been impossible to move more than 4,000 men.

And everything goes to show that matters were not much further forward in this field on the other side of the Atlantic either.

Moreover, it must be admitted that it would be hard to find a less suitable base from which to mount an invasion of the Continent than the Cherbourg peninsula, which was quite appropriately known in the Middle Ages as the "Cotentin enclosure". Its base is effectively cut off by a network of small rivers, marshes, and fields, which can easily be flooded by the operation of two or three sluice-gates. Nothing would have been easier for the enemy, once he had recovered from his initial surprise, than to block the paths of exit from the peninsula at its narrowest point – on the right at Carentan and on the left at Lessay.

These were the arguments which Churchill and Brooke persuasively and validly pressed against their American allies. And, apart from all these matters, it is undeniable that the British were naturally resistant to any such strategy as that proposed by General Marshall. For the British military authorities remained, on doctrinal grounds, as opposed to the teachings of Clausewitz and Napoleon as are British jurists to the legal code of Justinian. There were also the lessons of World War I to be taken into account. Nineteen months of war in 1917–1918 had cost only 50,510 American lives, and the United States entered World War II without their taste for offensive action tempered in the least. For the British, matters were quite different. On the Western Front alone they had lost 684,000 men between August 5, 1914, and November 11, 1918, and often these men were lost in engagements which offered little chance of success. Hence Churchill and Brooke sought to achieve a relatively easy initial victory which was clearly not to be had between the Cape de la Hague and Barfleur Point.

Churchill accepts the American plan

Until now the British Prime Minister and his C.I.G.S. had been as one. But scarcely had General Brooke succeeded in thwarting what he believed to be the disastrous Operation "Sledgehammer" than Churchill laid before him another, code-

General Sir Hastings Ismay, chief-of-staff to Churchill in the latter's capacity as Minister of Defence, played an immensely important and often overlooked part in the successful prosecution of the war. Ismay was born in 1887, and in World War I served only in Somaliland, his requests for transfer to a more active theatre being constantly refused. After the war he became an administrative soldier, and in 1939 he was head of the Secretariat of the Committee of Imperial Defence. As Churchill's subordinate he interpreted the latter's instructions and liaised with the Chiefs-of-Staff Committee.

△ *Harry Hopkins, whose advice was always listened to with great respect by President Roosevelt.*

△ A U.S. paratrooper in training. Invasions across the sea were to prove the great importance of airborne troops to secure an initial foothold in enemy-held territory and in capturing and holding centres of communication until relieved by more orthodox units.

named "Jupiter". The aim of this project was to capture the aerodromes from which German bombers took off to harass the Allies' Arctic convoys.

"If we could gain possession of these airfields and establish an equal force there not only would the Northern sea route to Russia be kept open, but we should set up a second front on a small scale from which it would be most difficult to eject us. If the going was good we could advance gradually southward, unrolling the Nazi map of Europe from the top. All that has to be done is to oust the enemy from the airfields and destroy their garrisons."

The Chiefs-of-Staff were not impressed by the Prime Minister's reasoning, and on July 13 he came back to his theme in a memorandum which, while purely formal in composition, manifested clear signs of considerable irritation.

"The following note on 'Jupiter' should be read by the Planning Committee in conjunction with my previous paper on the subject. The Planners should set themselves to making a positive plan and overcoming the many difficulties, and not concern themselves with judging whether the operation is desirable or not, which must be decided by higher authority."

Despite this rebuff, "Jupiter" turned out as still-born as "Sledgehammer". And for very good reason, as the conquest of

the German air bases was even less realisable than the attack on Trondheim which the Chiefs-of-Staff had vetoed in the previous autumn.

Among other considerations, one of the most powerful was that successful provision of air cover for the amphibious forces to be used in the assault depended on a number of somewhat tenuous assumptions. Churchill in fact thought that he could provide this support by basing six fighter and two or three bomber squadrons at Murmansk, but it now seems that this supposed too optimistic an assessment of the logistic possibilities which that base then offered.

Churchill meets Roosevelt...

Be this as it may, on June 17, Winston Churchill and his C.I.G.S. flew to Washington to finalise the Anglo-American strategy for 1942 and 1943. In the American capital, however, neither Roosevelt nor Harry Hopkins harboured any further illusions about still being able to convert their ally to the establishment of a second front in Europe in the autumn. Yet neither of them was disposed to keep the American troops destined for this purpose on an idle war footing until "Round-up" in spring 1943, and even less were they ready to see them used for operations in the Pacific theatre, as Admiral King had suggested. So if the principle of "Germany first" were to be adhered to, a principle which formed the keystone of White House policy, Operation "Gymnast" would have to be revived, even though the Hopkins-Marshall mission in April had given it scant attention.

. . . and persuades him to accept "Gymnast"

And this is indeed what happened, although one may say that it happened somewhat obliquely. For on July 21 it was agreed between the English and Americans, without however committing themselves to any definite decision, that Winston Churchill's favourite project should be re-examined. As the last paragraph of General Ismay's minute at the conclusion of the meeting records:

"The possibilities of French North Africa (Operation 'Gymnast') will be explored carefully and conscientiously, and plans will be completed in all details as soon as possible. Forces to be employed in 'Gymnast' would in the main be found from 'Bolero' units which have not yet left the United States . . . Planning of 'Bolero' will continue to be centred in London. Planning for 'Gymnast' will be centred in Washington." On the same day Churchill met Eisenhower.

"At five o'clock therefore Major-Generals Eisenhower and Clark were brought to my air-cooled room. I was immediately impressed by these remarkable but hitherto unknown men. They had both come from the President, whom they had just seen for the first time. We talked almost entirely about the major cross-Channel invasion in 1943, 'Round-up' as it was then called, on which their thoughts had evidently been concentrated. We had a most agreeable discussion, lasting for over an hour... At that time I thought of the spring or summer of 1943 as the date for the attempt. I felt sure that these officers were intended to play a great part in it, and that was the reason why they had been sent to make my acquaintance."

The battle for Roosevelt's assent for "Gymnast" had now been won, but he still had to convince General Marshall and Admiral King, who were not yet fully persuaded of the wisdom of this very considerable change of plan. To this end Roosevelt sent them both to London under the leadership of his confidant Harry Hopkins to undertake a final examination of the situation together with the American military mission stationed in London and with his ally's Chiefs-of-Staff. And on Saturday, July 18, beside the Thames, they met Generals Eisenhower and Spaatz and Admiral Stark.

Marshall and King finally consent

In appearance all options were still open, but only in appearance. For it was now scarcely possible to complete the preparations necessary for a cross-Channel descent on the Cherbourg peninsula before the September equinox. After that date local weather conditions might very well make the whole enterprise impossible for weeks on end. On this point American naval experts were no less pessimistic than their British colleagues, and in *The White House Papers of Harry Hopkins* Robert Sherwood has well summarised the discussion which finally settled the issue. "There was sufficient unanimity on the British side and a large enough fragment of doubt on the American side to make it impossible to push through the agreement for SLEDGEHAMMER."

Foreseeing this check, President Roosevelt, in one of the orders he had signed as Commander-in-Chief, expressly put out of court the Pacific venture favoured by General Marshall and Admiral King. And they were then asked to choose between reinforcing the British Army in the Middle East with American troops and attempting a landing in French North Africa under American command.

Naturally enough, Marshall and King opted for the second alternative, which was ratified by an inter-Allied agreement on July 24, 1942. But since the plans for Operation "Gymnast" had seen the inside of too many offices since the "Arcadia" Conference, it was decided to rechristen it Operation "Torch" for reasons of security. It was planned that this operation should be launched under the command of Eisenhower sometime before October 30.

Meanwhile, contact with the French authorities in North Africa favourable to the Allies was to be established.

△ *A cynical German view of Allied co-operation: Roosevelt, Stalin and Churchill in unison, "We shall form a wonderful brotherhood of peoples." But each to himself, "Only as long as we need each other."*
Overleaf: *the main threat to the Allies' arctic convoys, the superb German battleship* Tirpitz, *photographed from the heavy cruiser* Hipper. *As long as* Tirpitz *was in Norwegian waters, the Royal Navy had to keep a force capable of taking her on concentrated in Scapa Flow.*

According to Soviet historians, not only had their Anglo-Saxon allies broken their promise to the Soviet Union to open a second front in Europe but also done no better when it came to furnishing the arms, equipment, petrol, and raw materials which shortly after Hitler's invasion Russia had been assured of receiving.

But it is only proper to note that this accusation can only be made to stand up by comparing the number of tanks, planes etc. that Churchill and Roosevelt had promised to Stalin with those that actually arrived in Russia, while in justice the comparison ought to be made between the quantities promised and those which were embarked in American and British ports. For what was lost *en route* can scarcely be attributed to bad faith on the part of London or Washington. To get such supplies to the Soviet Union, Britain and America had the choice of three routes:

1. They could go via Vladivostok, through which Britain, before Pearl Harbor, could send sizable quantities of tin and rubber from Malaya to Siberia. After the opening of hostilities in the Far East, as we have noted, the Japanese did not stop Russian vessels plying between Vladivostok and America's Pacific ports. However, the Trans-Siberian Railway was capable at this time of carrying little more than it had been able to do at the beginning of the century.

2. There was the Persian Gulf route, which had become available on the occupation of Persia by Anglo-Soviet forces at the end of August 1941. This gave them control of the rail and road links between the Persian Gulf and the Caspian Sea. But supplies flowed along these two lines very feebly and thought was now given to making significant improvements in them by sending out a large contingent of American engineers and technicians. Nevertheless, the Allied merchantmen taking this route and sailing from New York or Liverpool still had to round the Cape of Good Hope, which put the American Atlantic ports at a distance of 73 days from Bandar-e-Shāhpur on the Persian Gulf.

3. Lastly, there was the Arctic route to Archangel and Murmansk. Situated on the estuary of the northern Dvina at the southern edge of the White Sea, the first of these two ports is inaccessible in winter and, anyway, was badly equipped in 1942. The other, thanks to the Gulf Stream, is open all the year round and, given the

Smoke belches up from a stricken
merchantman, only to be whipped
away by the savage winds so
prevalent in the high latitudes
through which the Allied
convoys had to sail to Russia.
The photograph could be of a
convoy anywhere in northern
waters, but it should be
remembered that exposure to
Arctic temperatures in these
latitudes resulted in death from
exposure in under five minutes.

942

circumstances, was somewhat better fitted out. It was, however, dangerously exposed to heavy air attack from the Luftwaffe.

During the winter, Allied Arctic convoys benefited from the cover of the long Arctic night. On the other hand, the advance of pack ice towards the south forced them to round North Cape at a distance which laid them open to short-range German attacks. In summer, the retreat of the ice allowed the convoys to stand further off from the Norwegian coast, but for 24 hours out of 24 they were, if discovered, an easy prey to dive-bomber, torpedo aircraft, and submarine attacks.

On the outward journey these convoys were distinguished by the letters P.Q. followed by their sequence number. The ships, which were unloaded at Murmansk and Archangel, waited there until they were numerous enough to be regrouped as a Q.P. convoy, and raised anchor when the escort ships of an incoming convoy could accompany them on the voyage home.

The first Arctic convoys

Convoy P.Q.1 set sail from Scottish waters on September 29, 1941, and before the end of the year five others had followed it, landing in all 120,000 tons of supplies at Murmansk, including 600 tanks, 800 aircraft, and 1,400 motor vehicles. Opponents of Winston Churchill's war strategy claim that these supplies would have sufficed to check the Japanese at Singapore and to defeat Rommel at Tobruk. Whatever the truth of this assertion, it has to be admitted that the Germans found themselves considerably embarrassed by these first convoys, which they had not foreseen. It is also noteworthy that between September 28 and December 31, 1941, all 55 vessels of the first six convoys reached their destination safely.

During the first half of 1942 no less than ten convoys made the Arctic run, and of their 146 cargo vessels, 128 reached port despite the increasing opposition of the German Navy. As we have already seen, Hitler had feared an Anglo-American landing in Norway and in consequence had stationed the 43,000-ton battleship *Tirpitz*, the pocket battleships *Lützow* and *Admiral Scheer*, the heavy cruiser *Admiral Hipper*, and a dozen U-boats between Trondheim and Narvik. And, at the return of spring, *Luftflotte* V had at its bases around the North Cape more than

△ ◁ *In an otherwise peaceful scene, an Allied tanker blows up in the midst of an Arctic convoy. Such tankers were always an enigma, for hit by a bomb or torpedo, a tanker would either explode almost immediately or burn for an indefinite time before being saved or sinking.*
△ ◁ ◁ *A British seaman keeps watch over the merchantmen of an Allied convoy to Russia during one of the long twilights of October 1942. Note the captive balloons being flown as anti-aircraft defences.*
▽ ◁ ◁ *The British armed trawler* Ayrshire *in Hvalfjord before sailing to join Convoy P.Q. 17. Ayrshire, of 540 tons, was typical of the deep sea trawlers requisitioned by the Admiralty in 1939 as escorts in northern waters.*
▽ ◁ *The British destroyer* Faulkner *lays a smokescreen during a Russian convoy. Smoke-screens, however, were efficient only against surface attacks, whereas most attacks on the Russian convoys were delivered by aircraft and submarines.*

△ *Colonel-General Hans Jürgen Stumpff, whose* Luftflotte V, *from its bases in Norway, had the task of spotting and then attacking the Allied convoys making for the Russian ports of Murmansk and Archangel.*

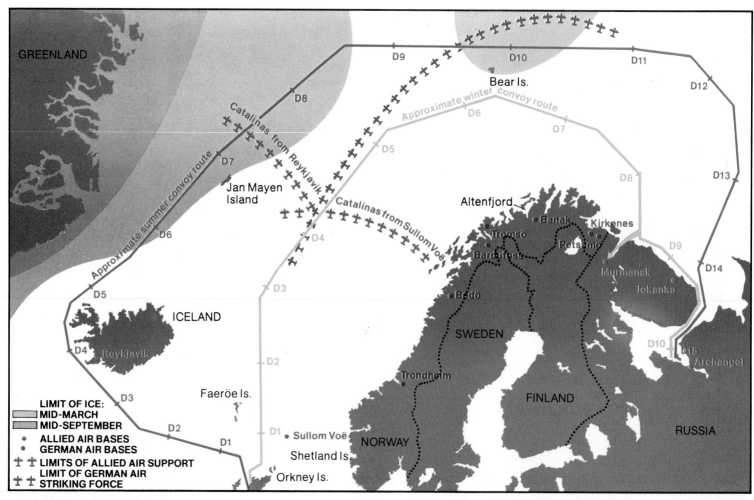

250 machines, including 130 Junkers Ju 87 and 88 bombers and 60 land and seaplane torpedo aircraft.

Faced by this concentration of forces, the Admiralty was forced to provide the same protection for the Arctic convoys as for the Mediterranean ones. Yet at the same time it was the Admiralty which had to bear the brunt of the battle of the Atlantic – and after having just improvised another fleet for the Far East.

In consequence, the situation was very precarious, especially since Roosevelt continued to urge Churchill to intensify and speed up the provisioning of the Soviet Union. And to this end he attached Task Force 99 (Rear-Admiral R. C. Giffen) to the Home Fleet, with two 35,000-ton battleships, the aircraft-carrier *Wasp*, two heavy cruisers, and a flotilla of destroyers.

At the beginning of March *Tirpitz* came out to intercept and destroy the convoys P.Q. 12 and Q.P. 8, a total of 31 cargo vessels, but because of inadequate aerial reconnaissance the powerful battleship failed to locate her prey. The hunter now became the hunted, since the Home Fleet, which had been detailed to provide strategic cover for the operation, had not failed to notice *Tirpitz*'s movements; and

on the morning of March 9 she was attacked by 12 torpedo-planes from *Victorious*. However, the undeniable bravery of the Fleet Air Arm pilots did not make up for their lack of training. None of the torpedoes hit its target.

Success for the Luftwaffe

The next convoy to arrive at Murmansk, between March 30 and April 1, lost five ships on the way. The U-boats and the Luftwaffe claimed two each, and the fifth went to a division of destroyers which had put out from the port of Kirkenes. But the Germans paid for this success with the loss of the destroyer *Z-26* and the U-boats *U-585* and *U-655*. In the course of the encounter that led to the sinking of *Z-26* the British cruiser *Trinidad* was damaged by one of her own torpedoes and had to put into Murmansk.

At the end of April the protection of P.Q. 15, with its 15 merchant vessels, occasioned the loss of the cruiser *Edinburgh*, torpedoed by *U-450* and finished off two days later by destroyer attack. For its part, *Trinidad* left Murmansk again only

◁ *The Russian convoy route. Unlike the Atlantic convoy routes, this was circumscribed by the ice to the north and the range of land-based aircraft to the south.*
◁◁▽ *Always the same lesson for convoys. But even if total secrecy was maintained in Great Britain, the Russian convoys were almost invariably discovered in the "straits" between the ice and Norway.*
◁▽ *The same message, different words.*
▽ *A British destroyer picks up survivors of an Arctic convoy from the light cruiser* Scylla *late in 1942.*
Overleaf: *"A British convoy on its way to Russia, 1942" by Charles Pears.*

△ *An octuple 2-pdr "pom-pom" anti-aircraft gun on a British warship. This was one of the Royal Navy's most efficient weapons, and could throw up an enormous volume of fire against enemy aircraft.*
▽ *A victim, in the form of a Focke-Wulf Fw 200 Condor. It was these aircraft, with their considerable range, that were one of the main bugbears of the Arctic convoys. Only rarely did they venture within the range of Allied anti-aircraft fire, preferring to stay out of range and report from there.*

to be sunk by a Junkers Ju 88, and to crown misfortunes, in the fog, the battleship *King George V* attacked the destroyer *Punjabi*, which sank within a few minutes, though not before her exploding depth-charges had damaged *King George V* severely.

As the days lengthened the losses of the convoys mounted, despite the reinforcement of their escorts with anti-aircraft vessels bristling with A.A. guns, and C.A.M. ships, merchantmen from which a Hurricane fighter could be catapulted into the air. Of the 35 vessels that made up P.Q. 16, which set sail from the base at Hvalfjord, north of Reykjavik, seven fell into the ambushes prepared for them by the Luftwaffe and U-boats, with losses that have been tabulated by Captain S. W. Roskill as follows:

	Loaded	Lost
Tons	125,000	32,400
Tanks	468	147
Aircraft	201	77
Vehicles	3,277	770

However disappointing they may have been, these losses were slight when compared with the catastrophe which overtook P.Q. 17, a disaster not only on account of the strength of the attack to which it succumbed, but also because of

the unfortunate intervention of the First Lord of the Admiralty, Admiral of the Fleet Sir Dudley Pound.

Convoy P.Q. 17 was composed of 35 vessels, 22 of which were American, eight British, two Russian, two Panamanian, and one Dutch. It set sail from the Bay of Reykjavik on June 27, 1942, with an escort of six destroyers, four corvettes, four armed trawlers, three mine-sweepers, two submarines and two auxiliary anti-aircraft vessels. Further support was given by Rear-Admiral L. H. K. Hamilton's squadron, which comprised four heavy cruisers, two of which were American, and three destroyers. Finally, Admiral Sir John Tovey had ordered the Home Fleet to sea, bringing together under his command the battleships *Duke of York* and *Washington* (U.S.N.), the aircraft-carrier *Victorious*, the cruisers *Nigeria* and *Cumberland*, and 14 destroyers. The Admiralty had done things in style.

Discovered on July 1, the convoy lost three merchant vessels on July 4, all to torpedoes dropped by German Heinkel 111's. By the evening of that same day the convoy was still about 280 miles away from Archangel by way of the North Cape – for Murmansk had been almost completely destroyed by repeated bomber

The British C.A.M. ship *Empire Faith*

The main features of the concept are readily
visible: a ramp on the bows of a merchantman,
down which the Hurricane could be catapulted
in an emergency. After flight the aircraft had to
ditch in the sea.

The British Flower-class corvette *Anchusa*

Displacement: 925 tons.
Armament: one 4-inch, one 2-pdr or four
.5-inch, and four .303-inch guns.
Speed: 16 knots.
Length: 205 feet.
Beam: 33 feet.
Draught: $11\frac{1}{2}$ feet.
Complement: 85.

The German Type IXB U-boat

Displacement: 1,051/1,178 tons.
Armament: one 4.1-inch, one 3.7-cm, and one
2-cm gun, plus six torpedo tubes with 22
torpedoes, or six torpedoes and 42 mines.
Speed: $18\frac{1}{4}/7\frac{3}{4}$ knots.
Range: 8,700 miles at 12 knots/64 miles at 4 knots.
Length: 251 feet. **Beam:** $22\frac{1}{4}$ feet.
Draught: 15 feet.
Complement: 48.

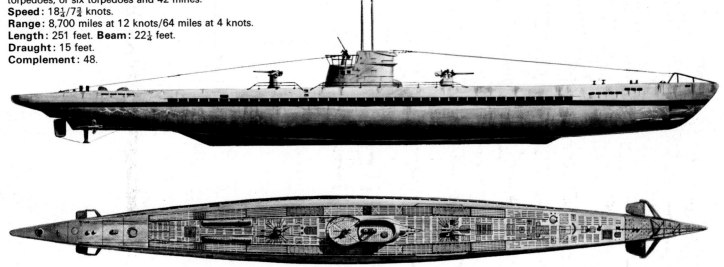

"MOST IMMEDIATE. CRUISER FORCE WITHDRAW TO WESTWARD AT HIGH SPEED.
"IMMEDIATE. OWING TO THREAT OF SURFACE SHIPS CONVOY IS TO
 DISPERSE AND PROCEED TO RUSSIAN PORTS.
"MOST IMMEDIATE. MY 2123 OF THE 4TH. CONVOY IS TO SCATTER."

△ A peaceful scene, little indicative of the disaster that was so soon to follow: a German aerial reconnaissance photograph of Convoy P.Q. 17 early on its fated passage.

◁◁ Air-sea warfare in the bleak northern waters of the Barents Sea: a Heinkel 111 bomber roars past a merchantman after releasing its torpedo. In these northern waters convoys were always in dire straits once they had been spotted, for the sea room available to them was circumscribed by the ice to the north and German-occupied Norway to the south.

◁△ One of P.Q. 17's merchantmen sinking, photographed from the U-boat responsible for her loss.

◁▽ Survivors from the American ship Carlton, photographed from the U-boat which had sunk their vessel on July 5, 1942.

△▷ Typical conditions on a calm day in Arctic waters. After the disastrous "scatter" order given to P.Q. 17, the captain of the trawler Ayrshire collected three merchantmen together and took them 20 miles into the ice. There they painted their upper works white to blend with their surroundings, and remained unscathed for two days until July 7, when they headed for Novaya Zemlya.

▷ A British warship in action.

ARMS FOR RUSSIA . . . A great convoy of British ships escorted by Soviet fighter planes sails into Murmansk harbour with vital supplies for the Red Army.

△ △ *The Russian port of Murmansk under German bombing attack. This primary port for Allied arctic convoys was unfortunately only a few miles up the Kola Inlet on Russia's Barents Sea coast, and well within the range of bombers from the German airfields at Petsamo and Kirkenes.*

△ *A British poster extols the co-operation of British and Soviet forces in getting a convoy through to Russia.*

attacks by *Luftflotte* V.

The Admiralty was now informed that *Tirpitz* had joined *Scheer* and *Hipper* in Altenfjord, which led to the inference that a powerful enemy formation would attack the convoy and Rear-Admiral Hamilton's supporting escort around dawn next day and would swiftly destroy them. Upon which, after brief deliberation, Sir Dudley Pound sent out these three messages, which sealed the convoy's fate.

"2111 Hours: Most immediate. Cruiser force withdraw to westward at high speed.

"2123 Hours: Immediate. Owing to the threat of surface ships convoy is to disperse and proceed to Russian ports.

"2136 Hours: Most Immediate. My 2123 of the 4th. Convoy is to scatter."

On receiving these orders Rear-Admiral Hamilton retired at the indicated speed, taking with him the six escort destroyers. The convoy dispersed as ordered. But of the 30 merchantmen which were left to make Archangel by themselves only 11 arrived at their destination between July 11 and July 25, some of them having made off eastwards towards Novaya Zemlya to escape their pursuers. Nine cargo ships fell prey to air attack from *Luftflotte* V and ten to the 82 torpedoes fired by the U-boats involved. The Germans lost only two bombers, three torpedo planes, and two reconnaissance aircraft.

Tirpitz and her companions, escorted by six destroyers, left Altenfjord at 1100

hours on July 5, more than 12 hours after Hitler had given his permission. But they did not get far, for the same day, at 2200 hours, they were ordered to return to base immediately.

As may be expected, this tragic episode gave rise to passionate dispute in Great Britain, and, as Captain Roskill judiciously points out, it is undeniable that in thinking it possible to give orders for action at a distance of 1,750 miles from his London base, the First Naval Lord had exceeded his competence. Certainly, Admiral Pound was a fine leader in every sense of the term, but as it turned out he was no better able to command by *Führerbefehl* than was Adolf Hitler himself.

The table of losses occasioned by the P.Q. 17 disaster is as follows:

	Loaded	Lost
Tons	156,492	99,316
Tanks	594	430
Aircraft	297	210
Vehicles	4,246	3,350

We may easily understand now that despite Stalin's exhortations, when faced with these figures, Winston Churchill should have waited until September before permitting P.Q. 18 to set out. And even though it was provided with a powerful escort – including the escort carrier *Avenger* – 13 of the 40 vessels that then sailed from Hvalfjord were lost. But on the German side losses were not light: four submarines and 41 aircraft.

CHAPTER 70
PEDESTAL: The worst Malta Convoy

It was on the afternoon of June 21, in the elegant White House study of President Roosevelt, that Winston Churchill first learnt of the fall of Tobruk. According to Churchill's memoirs, on learning of the catastrophe, the President dropped everything and immediately summoned General Marshall. Lord Alanbrooke, on the other hand, in the 1946 additions to his war diaries, would have us believe that it was General Marshall himself who delivered the bad news to the two statesmen, as they conferred in the Oval Room of the White House.

"I can remember this incident as if it had occurred yesterday. Churchill and I were standing beside the President's desk talking to him, when Marshall walked in with a pink piece of paper containing a message of the fall of Tobruk. Neither Winston nor I had contemplated such an eventuality and it was a staggering blow. I cannot remember what the actual words were that the President used to convey his sympathy, but I remember vividly being impressed by the tact and real heartfelt sympathy which lay behind these words. There was not one word too much nor one word too little."

But Roosevelt did not stop at mere eloquent expressions of sympathy; quite spontaneously, he immediately asked what he could do to temper the effects of the disaster inflicted upon the British Army. His first idea was to send out the American 1st Armoured Division to the Middle East, but the carrying out of such a project would have created enormous difficulties; he and General Marshall, therefore, in a spirit of comradeship rarely known in coalitions, offered to refit the 8th Army, by giving it the 300 Sherman tanks that had just been distributed to the American armoured units. To complete this most generous gift, 100 self-propelled 105-mm guns were also offered. But even that was not all, for when the cargo vessel carrying the 300 tank engines was torpedoed and sunk off Bermuda, "without a single word from us the President and Marshall put a further supply of engines into another fast ship and dispatched it to overtake the convoy. 'A friend in need is a friend indeed.'"

The entry into active service of the 31-ton M4 Sherman tank upgraded the hitting power of the 8th Army in the Battle of El Alamein. Its long-barrelled (37.5 cali-

△ *Axis forces outside Tobruk. It was the fall of this key British fortress, of whose loss Churchill was informed on June 21, that prompted President Roosevelt to make the generous transfer of 300 Sherman tanks and 100 M7 105-mm self-propelled guns to the British. And though these would not be available in time for the Battle of Alam el Halfa, they would be ready for the decisive Battle of El Alamein.*

bre) 75-mm gun was almost as good as the shorter (24 calibre) 7.5-cm gun generally fitted to the heaviest tanks (the Pzkw IV) of the *Panzerarmee Afrika*; secondly it had a less obtrusive shape than its predecessor, the M3 Grant; finally, the latter's awkward sponson was replaced in the Sherman tank by a turret capable of traversing through 360 degrees.

For diplomatic reasons it was not revealed at the time that the Sherman was what General Sir Brian Horrocks, commander of XIII Corps at El Alamein, later in his memoirs called "a brilliant example of Anglo-American co-operation". American engineers were in charge of the tank's mechanical features (engine, transmission, and tracks), whilst the armament derived from researches carried out by a British team. It was, apparently, because he wanted the aid the Americans were so generously giving to receive full public recognition, that Churchill suppressed the extent of British participation.

R.A.F. reinforcements

At the same time (summer 1942), the Italo-German air forces fighting in North Africa finally lost their last remnants of superiority over the R.A.F., now being regularly reinforced by deliveries of American and British aircraft, which, technically and tactically, were of the highest quality: there was, for example, the Supermarine Spitfire Mark V interceptor and the Hawker Hurricane IID fighter-bomber, nicknamed the "tin-opener", because its 40-mm armour-piercing shells tore through the thickest Panzer armour with considerable ease. Later came the excellent North American P-51 Mustang fighter capable of 390 mph, and with a ceiling of 31,000 feet. Roosevelt's sympathetic understanding of Britain's needs also made it possible to increase to 117 the number of strategic bombers posted to this theatre, when the four-engined American Consolidated B-24 Liberator bomber joined the British-built Handley-Page Halifax.

It therefore follows that the R.A.F. not only recovered, conclusively and permanently, mastery of the air, but also that it was able to give the 8th Army, in both its defensive and offensive rôles, support that daily became more powerful and better organised. In his book on the war in the air, Air Vice-Marshal J. E. Johnson has

traced this development very precisely:

"Slowly, by trial, error, and the foresight of gifted men, not only airmen, the pattern of air support for the soldiers again took shape. Fighters to grind down the enemy bomber and fighter forces; fighters which could then be armed with bombs to attack the enemy ground forces; fighters which, armed or not with bombs, were always capable of protecting themselves and providing protection for the bombers. A bomber force which was as capable of bombing enemy airfields and installations as of attacking troops on the ground. A reconnaissance force to be the eyes of both Army and Air Force Commanders."

Among the "gifted men" whom the author mentions, pride of place must go to General Bernard Law Montgomery, who on taking over command of the 8th Army, set up his H.Q. next to that of Air Vice-Marshal Coningham, commanding the Desert Air Force, as the Middle East's tactical air force was called.

Churchill decides that Auchinleck must go

We have already seen that, since June 25, General Sir Claude Auchinleck had been

△ ◁ *Auchinleck meets Churchill on the latter's arrival in Cairo.*
▽ ◁ *An American M4 Sherman tank. Although a considerable improvement on the Grant and contemporary British tanks, the Sherman still left much to be desired in comparison with the latest German armoured fighting vehicles, especially in gun power.*
△ *Churchill addresses some of the ever growing number of British troops in the Middle East. He told such men of how the Shermans they were about to receive "had been longed and thirsted for by the 1st United States Armoured Division, and how they had been taken from them ... in order to give us the chance—or perhaps I said the certainty—of saving Alexandria, Cairo, and Egypt from conquest."*
◁ *The meeting of "All The Talents" in Cairo. Left to right, standing: Tedder, Brooke, Harwood, and R. G. Casey; sitting: Smuts, Churchill, Auchinleck, and Wavell.*

955

at the head of both the 8th Army and the Middle East Land Forces, a situation of which Churchill fully approved, as is shown by his message of June 28; and on July 4, when he learnt that the 8th Army was not only standing its ground, but even counter-attacking, he again showed his satisfaction: "I must tell you how pleased I am with the way things are shaping," he wrote that day. "If fortune turns I am sure you will press your advantage, as you say, 'relentlessly'."

And yet, three weeks later, Churchill had decided, if not actually to dismiss him, at least to deprive him of his command in Egypt, Palestine, and Syria, thus limiting him to Iraq and Persia. Quite clearly, Churchill was once more itching to attack, whereas lack of resources, and the need to wait for the reinforcements which were coming around the Cape of Good Hope, made G.H.Q. Cairo wish to refrain from any large-scale offensive initiative until mid-September. And when it is realised that an 8th Army counter-offensive of July 27 came unstuck because of land-mines, and that the new command team of Alexander and Montgomery waited until October 23 before attacking, it is difficult not to accept the point of view of the Cairo command.

Auchinleck's psychology erroneous?

On the other hand General Brooke, whose sturdy independence vis-à-vis Churchill is well known, never stopped saying, in his war diaries, that "It was quite clear that something was radically wrong but not easy at a distance to judge what this something was, nor how far wrong it was . . . The crisis had now come and it was essential that I should go out to see what was wrong. But for this I wanted to be alone."

To help us interpret these somewhat veiled remarks, we have available the testimony of three very different personalities: Field-Marshal Smuts, the Prime Minister of South Africa, Field-Marshal Montgomery, and General Sir Alexander Galloway (who served in Egypt in 1940 and 1941). They all criticised Sir Claude Auchinleck for an inability to choose his subordinate officers. Montgomery expressed himself on this subject with his usual directness.

"A good judge of men would never have selected General Corbett to be his Chief of Staff in the Middle East. And to suggest that Corbett should take command of the Eighth Army, as Auchinleck did, passed all comprehension.

"Again, nobody in his senses would have sent Ritchie to succeed Cunningham in command of the Eighth Army; Ritchie had not the experience or qualifications for the job and in the end he had to be removed too." A brutal judgement, certainly, but one which corresponds with General Galloway's, when the latter pointed out that the former C.-in-C. Middle East Land Forces was incapable of deciding whether a man was really equal to the task demanded of him; and on August 4, 1942, Smuts had spoken in a similar vein to General Brooke in Cairo.

Alexander takes over from Auchinleck

At all events, the C.I.G.S., General Brooke, went to Cairo, inspecting Gibraltar and Malta on the way–but not alone, as he would have liked; Churchill had also

Reinforcements for Coningham's Western Desert Air Force were now beginning to arrive in considerable quantities, and the R.A.F. was able to wrest command of the skies from the Luftwaffe and Regia Aeronautica.
△ ◁ *A Spitfire VB interceptor and fighter-bomber. Though its speed was reduced when the Vokes air filter necessary for operations in the Middle East was fitted, it was still capable of besting the Italian and German fighters operating over the Western Desert.*
▽ ◁ *The bomb aimer's position of a Martin Baltimore light bomber. This aircraft was a development of the same company's Maryland, and served exclusively in the Middle East, serving with seven R.A.F. and two South African Air Force squadrons from March 1942.*
▽ *R.A.F. armourers bomb up a flight of Baltimores.*

▽ The extraordinary British battleship Rodney, *together with her sister ship* Nelson, *was the result of the Washington Naval Treaty. Displacement restrictions dictated that the main armament be grouped together forward, so that less weighty armour plate need be used.*

decided to go out and see for himself what the situation was like, and had summoned General Wavell, C.-in-C. India, and Field-Marshal Smuts, both men whose opinion he valued, to meet him in Cairo.

"Had General Auchinleck or his staff lost the confidence of the Desert Army? If so, should he be relieved, and who could succeed him?" According to his memoirs, these were the two big questions that brought Churchill to Cairo, where he landed on the morning of August 4, only a few minutes before the C.I.G.S. In reality his mind was already made up, as is proved by the fact that on August 6, at dawn, he went to see Brooke, just as the latter was getting up ("practically naked"), and told him that he had decided to split the Middle East theatre into two. Relegated to Basra or Baghdad, Auchinleck would be given the new Persia and Iraq Command, separated from the rest of Middle East Command, which Churchill now offered to Brooke. The latter asked not to be appointed on the grounds that this was no time to disorganise the Imperial General Staff, and that in any case

he had no knowledge of desert warfare. But that evening he confided to his diary:

"Another point which I did not mention was that, after working with the P.M. for close on nine months, I do feel at last that I can exercise a limited amount of control on some of his activities and that at last he is beginning to take my advice. I feel, therefore, that, tempting as the offer is, by

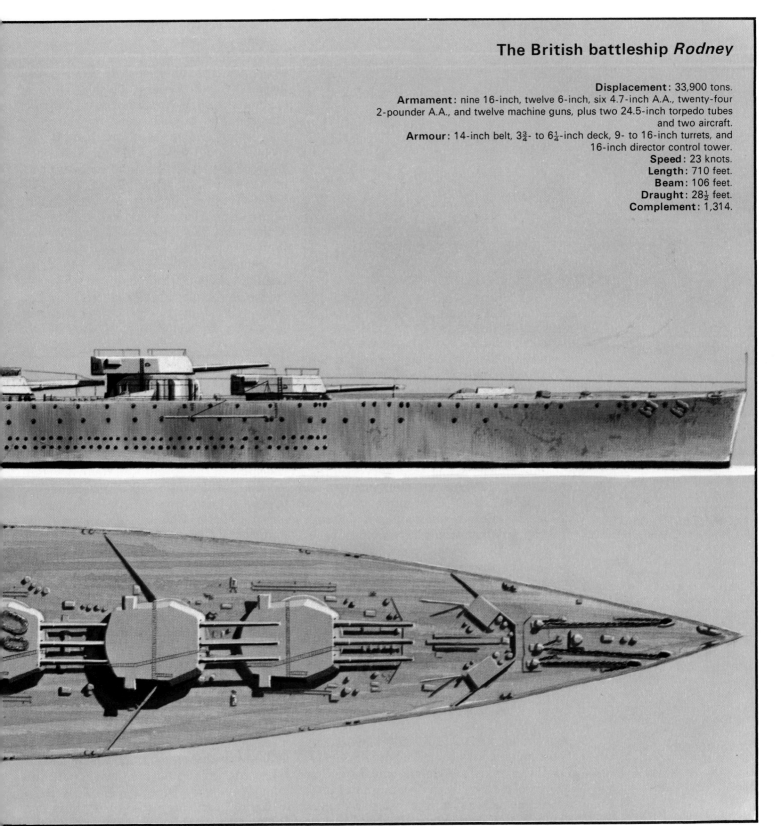

The British battleship *Rodney*

Displacement: 33,900 tons.
Armament: nine 16-inch, twelve 6-inch, six 4.7-inch A.A., twenty-four 2-pounder A.A., and twelve machine guns, plus two 24.5-inch torpedo tubes and two aircraft.
Armour: 14-inch belt, $3\frac{3}{4}$- to $6\frac{1}{4}$-inch deck, 9- to 16-inch turrets, and 16-inch director control tower.
Speed: 23 knots.
Length: 710 feet.
Beam: 106 feet.
Draught: $28\frac{1}{2}$ feet.
Complement: 1,314.

caused the plane to explode, leaving no survivors, and his successor, Brooke's candidate, took over and was told to get out to Cairo immediately. This was Lieutenant-General Bernard L. Montgomery – who had just introduced himself to Eisenhower as Alexander's successor as commander of the 1st Army. Small wonder that on being deprived of his second deputy in 48 hours, Eisenhower cynically asked "Are the British taking 'Torch' seriously?"

To replace General Corbett, Alexander chose as his chief-of-staff Lieutenant-General R. McCreery; he was a tank specialist, and Alexander wrote of him that "he was one of those officers who is as successful at H.Q. as at the head of his troops" and "faithful friend and companion" to him personally. Thus was formed the brilliant team which, with Air Chief-Marshal Sir Arthur Tedder and Admiral Sir Henry Harwood, led the 8th Army from El Alamein to Tripoli in less than nine months.

General Auchinleck, relieved of his command because he had refused to attack before mid-September, accepted his disgrace with dignity, but refused the consolation prize that Churchill offered.

Churchill's instructions

On August 10 the British Prime Minister, accompanied by Generals Wavell and Brooke, flew to Moscow to inform the Russians of the Anglo-American decision to abandon Operation "Sledgehammer" in favour of Operation "Torch". But before leaving Cairo, Churchill had sent Alexander hand-written instructions, fixing his tasks in the following manner:

"1. Your prime and main duty will be to take or destroy at the earliest opportunity the German-Italian Army commanded by Field-Marshal Rommel together with all its supplies and establishments in Egypt and Libya.

2. You will discharge or cause to be discharged such other duties as pertain to your command without prejudice to the task described in paragraph 1, which must be considered paramount in His Majesty's interests."

Contrast this message, containing what was essential and nothing more, with the long meandering Directive No. 41 written by Hitler in the previous April; these two documents enable us to measure the

General Sir Harold Alexander was born in 1891 and entered the British Army by means of Sandhurst. He served with great distinction with the Irish Guards in World War I and after the war in the Baltic States and in India. Alexander commanded the British rearguard at Dunkirk very ably, and further enhanced his reputation as G.O.C. Southern Command in 1940 and by his masterly retreat through Burma in 1942. He was then appointed Eisenhower's deputy for Operation "Torch", but was almost immediately asked to take over from Auchinleck in the Western Desert. With Montgomery commanding in the field, and Alexander in overall command, Rommel was pushed steadily back out of Egypt and Libya into Tunisia. February 1942 saw Alexander's appointment as Deputy Supreme Commander in North Africa and commander of the 18th Army Group. By May the Axis forces in Africa had been destroyed, and Alexander started planning the invasion of Italy.

accepting it I should definitely be taking a course which would on the whole help the war least. Finally, I could not bear the thought that Auchinleck might think that I had come out here on purpose to work myself into his shoes."

Brooke having thus refused, for the most honourable of reasons, Sir Harold Alexander was asked that very evening, on Brooke's recommendation, to take over the Middle East Command. A happy choice, for the new commander had shown the same imperturbability and resourcefulness at Dunkirk as later in the Burma jungle, and, in addition, wore his authority easily. "Calm, confident and charming – as always" was the impression the difficult Montgomery received on their first meeting at G.H.Q. Cairo. Alexander had just been appointed deputy to General Eisenhower, as commander of the British 1st Army taking part in "Torch", and Eisenhower now had to be asked to release him for this new post.

Originally, and in spite of Brooke's opposition, General W. H. E. Gott had been appointed to command the 8th Army, but the aircraft in which he was travelling was forced down by two German fighters; whilst he was helping other passengers caught in the wreckage, a second attack

The Italian Savoia-Marchetti 79-II ''*Sparviero*'' bomber

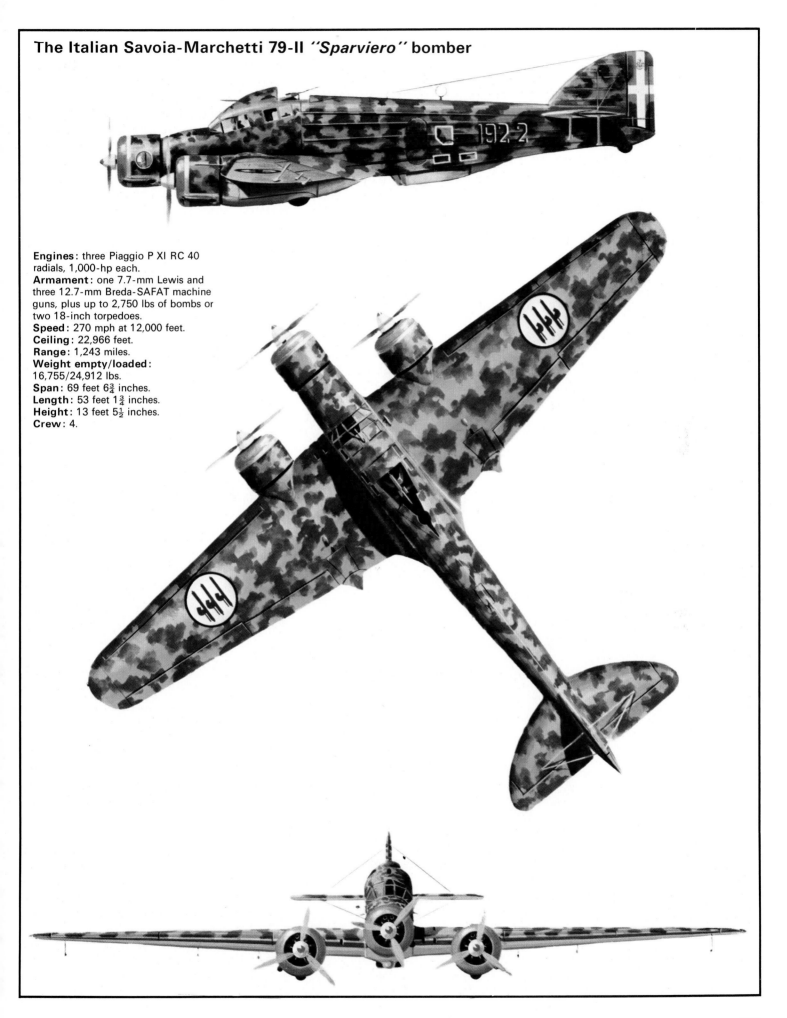

Engines: three Piaggio P XI RC 40 radials, 1,000-hp each.
Armament: one 7.7-mm Lewis and three 12.7-mm Breda-SAFAT machine guns, plus up to 2,750 lbs of bombs or two 18-inch torpedoes.
Speed: 270 mph at 12,000 feet.
Ceiling: 22,966 feet.
Range: 1,243 miles.
Weight empty/loaded: 16,755/24,912 lbs.
Span: 69 feet 6¾ inches.
Length: 53 feet 1¼ inches.
Height: 13 feet 5½ inches.
Crew: 4.

difference between the essential authority of the statesman, and the meddling despotism of the megalomaniac.

Operation "Pedestal"

Whilst Churchill and his advisers were setting off for Moscow via Teheran, 14 merchant ships slipped through the Strait of Gibraltar under cover of dense fog. The interruption of convoys to Archangel had allowed the Admiralty to devote considerable resources to this new operation of supplying Malta: three aircraft-carriers, *Eagle*, *Victorious*, and *Indomitable* with their 72 fighters; the two battleships *Nelson* and *Rodney*; seven cruisers, one of which was an anti-aircraft vessel; 24 destroyers; two tankers; four corvettes; and eight submarines. In addition, the old aircraft carrier *Furious*, with an escort of eight destroyers, was able to fly off 38 Spitfires to Malta. The convoy had 14 merchantmen.

This considerable naval force was under the overall command of Vice-Admiral Sir Neville Syfret, commanding Force H. Rear-Admiral H. M. Burrough, with four cruisers and 12 destroyers, was the convoy's immediate escort; bearing in mind what had happened the previous June, he

was to escort the convoy as far as Malta. Such were the outlines of "Pedestal".

However, it was all the more difficult to keep such a large-scale undertaking secret as the Italian secret service had paid informers in the Bay of Algeciras, and the Germans and Italians were able to prepare, right down to the smallest details, a plan to intercept and destroy the "Pedestal" convoy. This shows the close co-operation which now existed between *Supermarina*, under Admiral Arturo Riccardi, *Superaero* (General Rino Corso Fougier), and the Germans, Field-Marshal Kesselring and Admiral Weichold. However, they had to recognise that they would not be able to use the four battleships available to them, so great had the fuel crisis become since June 15. The attack would therefore be carried out by the following aerial and naval forces:

1. sixteen Italian and five German submarines, which would share the task of attacking the enemy between the Straits of Algiers and the Sicilian Channel with 784 aircraft (447 bombers, 90 torpedo aircraft, and 247 fighters);

2. eighteen motor torpedo boats, which would be lurking between Cap Bon and the island of Pantelleria; and

3. six cruisers and 11 destroyers which, in combination with the aerial forces, would finish off the convoy.

▽ *British light cruisers in action. Note the dual purpose 5.25-inch guns in the three two-gun turrets of the vessel in the foreground, and the smoke screen being laid by the further ship. Dual purpose guns were of vital importance in the Mediterranean, where the major attack, against which the main armament would be needed, might come from the sea or the air. Smoke screens were particularly effective against the Italian Navy as its vessels lacked radar and the smoke screen shielded the target from optical ranging.*
▷ ▽ *The aircraft-carrier* Indomitable, *severely damaged by three Stuka bomb hits, tries to struggle on as lighter British units steam round her in an effort to prevent further attacks.*
▷ *From top left to bottom right, the British carriers* Victorious, Indomitable, *and* Eagle, *whose fighters were to be the main defence against the heavy and determined Axis air attacks on the convoy and escort in the "Pedestal" operation. It was also to be the valiant* Eagle's *last mission.*

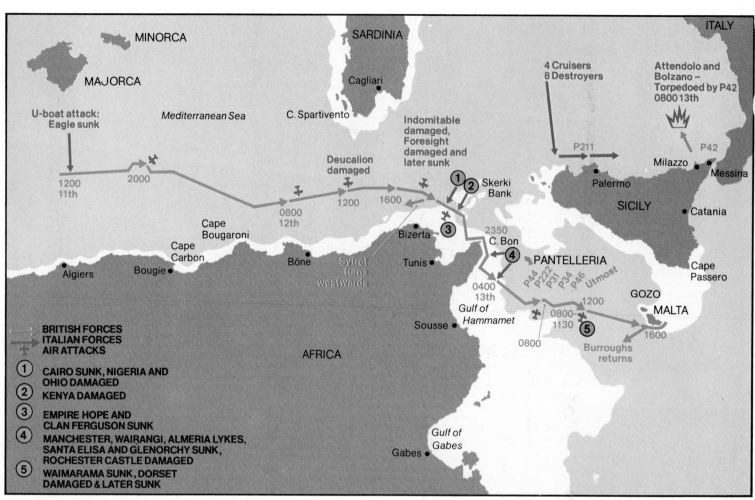

MINORCA

MAJORCA

U-boat attack:
Eagle sunk

Mediterranean Sea

1200
11th

2000

SARDINIA

Cagliari

C. Spartivento

ITALY

4 Cruisers
8 Destroyers

Attendolo and
Bolzano –
Torpedoed by P42
0800 13th

P211

P42

Milazzo

Messina

Deucalion
damaged

0800
12th

1200

1600

Indomitable
damaged,
Foresight
damaged and
later sunk

Skerki
Bank

①②

③

Palermo

SICILY

Catania

Cape
Bougaroni

Cape
Carbon

Algiers   Bougie

Bône

Bizerta

Tunis

*Syfret
turns
westwards*

2350
C. Bon

④

0400
13th

*Gulf of
Hammamet*

PANTELLERIA

Cape
Passero

P44 P202 P31 P34 P46 Utmost

0800–
1130

⑤

1200

GOZO

MALTA

1600

Sousse

AFRICA

0800

*Burroughs
returns*

BRITISH FORCES
ITALIAN FORCES
AIR ATTACKS

① **CAIRO SUNK, NIGERIA AND
OHIO DAMAGED**
② **KENYA DAMAGED**
③ **EMPIRE HOPE AND
CLAN FERGUSON SUNK**
④ **MANCHESTER, WAIRANGI, ALMERIA LYKES,
SANTA ELISA AND GLENORCHY SUNK,
ROCHESTER CASTLE DAMAGED**
⑤ **WAIMARAMA SUNK, DORSET
DAMAGED & LATER SUNK**

*Gulf of
Gabes*

Gabes

The Allies suffer

It was Lieutenant Rosenbaum (*U-73*) who opened the Axis score when, early on the afternoon of August 11, a salvo of four torpedoes struck the aircraft-carrier *Eagle*, and sank her in eight minutes, thus ending the career of this fine old ship, which had played so vital a part in the supplying of Malta. On the Axis side, a few hours later the destroyer *Wolverine* rammed and sank the Italian submarine *Dagabur* as it was trying to torpedo *Furious*, which, having accomplished her mission, was returning to Gibraltar.

Throughout August 12, the Hurricanes of the three aircraft-carriers repulsed successive attacks from some 200 dive-bombers and torpedo-carrying planes, which had taken off from the Sardinian bases of Elmas and Decimomannu; in conjunction with the anti-aircraft fire of the convoy, the Hurricanes destroyed 28 aircraft, so that during this second phase of the battle, the successes of the Axis air forces were meagre indeed: one cargo ship, damaged by a bomb, lagged behind the convoy and was finished off during the night by a motor torpedo boat, while three German Ju 87's scored hits on the flight deck of *Indomitable*, whose planes were then taken on board *Victorious*. The destroyer *Foresight*, which had received a torpedo hit, was scuttled by her own crew, while the destroyer *Ithuriel* sank the Italian submarine *Cobalto*.

At 1900 hours, having reached a point north of Bizerta, Syfret, in accordance with instructions, headed for Gibraltar with his support force, wishing Burrough and his convoy a safe journey, a wish which was never granted, for the third and fourth acts of this aero-naval tragedy firmly established the victory of the Axis forces, and especially the Italian Navy.

The last acts of the tragedy started just after 2000 hours, when, near Cape Bon, the two submarines *Axum* and *Dessié* (commanded by Lieutenants Ferrini and Scandola) fired eight torpedoes, five of which struck home, sinking the anti-aircraft cruiser *Cairo*, and causing serious damage to one of the convoy cargo ships (the tanker *Ohio*) and the cruiser *Nigeria*, Admiral Burrough's flagship. In the ensuing confusion a further air attack damaged two more merchant ships, which were sunk in the night by Italian naval forces. In addition, at about 2200 hours, the sub-

marine *Alagi* (Lieutenant Puccini) damaged the cruiser *Kenya* and sank yet another cargo ship. In the early hours of the 13th the Italian motor torpedo boats, prowling between Cap Bon and Pantelleria, fell upon the remnants of the convoy and attacked continuously until sunrise, sinking four more merchantmen and the cruiser *Manchester*.

Italy's last victory

But at the same time an equally fierce battle was being waged within the Axis Supreme Command, between Admirals Riccardi and Weichold on the one hand, and Field-Marshal Kesselring and General Fougier on the other; the question at issue was the following: on August 13, should the fighter cover be given to the two squadrons of cruisers charged with finishing off the convoy south of Pantelleria, or should they protect the bomber squadrons, since they would not be able to protect both at the same time?

Unable to decide between the two rival claims, Marshal Cavallero put the question to Mussolini, who decided that the

◁△ *Operation "Pedestal". Although escorted by very powerful British naval forces, the convoy of 14 merchantmen was harried almost to total loss by Axis aircraft and light naval forces. It was a story of skill and devotion on both sides, the Italians pressing home their torpedo attacks with great ability and courage, and the British forging on despite their losses in their effort to aid the island of Malta. Though British losses in this convoy could be likened to those of the ill-starred P.Q. 17, just enough supplies got through to tide the island over this last Axis effort.*
◁▽ *The* Dorset *ploughs on through a storm of bomb bursts.*
△ *Incredibly, the American tanker* Ohio *survived this torpedo hit and managed to get 10,000 tons of desperately needed fuel through to Malta.*
Overleaf: *"The Tanker* Ohio *in a Malta Convoy" by Norman Wilkinson.*

was intercepted on the way back to base by the submarine *Unbroken*, commanded by Lieutenant Alastair Mars, who scored two direct hits on the *Bolzano* and the *Attendolo*, damaging them so badly that they remained out of action till September 1943.

Bragadin's conclusion on this episode is that "the battle of mid-August 1942 marked the swan-song of the Italian Navy, and the last important victory of the Axis in the Mediterranean conflict". How right he was is seen from the fact that of the 85,000 tons of supplies loaded in the Clyde, 53,000 tons went to the bottom but the 32,000 tons that got through to Valletta were sufficient to see the island fortress through till November; and thanks to the admirable devotion to duty of Captain Dudley W. Mason and the crew of *Ohio*, which in impossible conditions managed to get through 10,000 tons of fuel, the torpedo planes and submarines stationed at Malta were able to engage their offensive against the Italian Navy with renewed vigour, until Rommel was finally and comprehensively defeated.

The end of Ohio's *great ordeal.* △ Ohio *approaches Grand Harbour with two British destroyers tied alongside to help keep her afloat.*

▽ *The end in sight – tugs ease the crippled tanker, her decks almost awash, into Valletta's Grand Harbour.*

fighters should protect the bombers: a bad decision as the Stuka bombers and torpedo planes sank only one ship, whereas the six cruisers and 11 motor torpedo boats originally due to go into action would almost certainly have finished off the five ships still left of the convoy. To make matters worse, the Italian naval squadron

CHAPTER 71

ALAM HALFA: Rommel's last throw

The last Panzer offensive towards Cairo, Alexandria, and the Suez Canal gave rise to two battles. The first was lost by Rommel between August 31 and September 5, 1942; the second, less conclusive, was the verbal battle fought after the war by Churchill and Montgomery on the one hand, and Auchinleck and his chief-of-staff (Major-General Dorman-Smith, who shared his chief's fall from grace in August 1942), on the other. This quarrel has been revived by Correlli Barnett who, in his book *The Desert Generals*, has passed harsh judgement on both the British Prime Minister and the victor of El Alamein. According to the latter, when he was received at Mena House on August 12, Auchinleck was anything but determined to defend the El Alamein position at all costs if there were an Italo-German offensive. Montgomery writes in his memoirs:

"He asked me if I knew he was to go. I said that I did. He explained to me his plan of operations; this was based on the fact that at all costs the Eighth Army was to be preserved 'in being' and must not be destroyed in battle. If Rommel attacked in strength, as was expected soon, the Eighth Army would fall back on the Delta; if Cairo and the Delta could not be held,

the army would retreat southwards up the Nile, and another possibility was a withdrawal to Palestine. Plans were being made to move the Eighth Army H.Q. back up the Nile."

Auchinleck has categorically denied ever having uttered such words to Montgomery, and since their conversation was private, there would be no way of settling the issue were it not for the fact that on his arrival in Cairo, General Alexander himself was struck by Auchinleck's insistence on keeping the 8th Army intact, the implication being that in certain circumstances, he had contemplated the possibility of withdrawing to the Delta, and had drawn up plans to that effect.

We cannot conclude from this, however, that Auchinleck would have deliberately retreated as soon as Rommel had begun his first large-scale manoeuvre, as Montgomery implies. On the contrary, everything seems to indicate that he fully intended to face up to an attack at El Alamein, in accordance with the plans drawn up by Major-General Dorman-Smith. Furthermore, it is fair to ask whether or not the new team at the head of the 8th Army, however determined it might be to fight, would have condemned it to destruction in the event of one of Rommel's typical out-flanking movements.

Was Dorman-Smith's plan, adopted by Auchinleck, taken over without reference or acknowledgement by Montgomery? This is the claim put forward by Correlli Barnett. In reality, such a plan was forced upon both generals by Rommel's probable tactics, and also by the nature of the terrain, which dominated the surrounding countryside by nearly 200 feet and did not lend itself to the German general's usual outflanking tactics. To this plan, however, Montgomery added personal qualities of dynamism and cunning, which justify him calling the plan his own.

Rommel forced to act precipitately

Faced with an opponent whom he knew to be getting stronger day by day, Rommel realised he had to attack, and quickly, otherwise he would soon be overrun by an opponent superior in numbers and equipment. He had been able to motorise his 90th Light Division, and had been rein-

Previous page: *A British infantryman, crouching behind cover improvised from stones, watches a burning German Kettenkrad, a semi-tracked motorcycle.*
▽ *General Montgomery surveys his dispositions from on top of a Crusader tank's turret. As soon as he had taken over from Auchinleck, Montgomery had started to alter his predecessor's plans, strengthening the left flank considerably. After the battle, Montgomery wrote: "My first encounter with Rommel was of great interest. Luckily I had time to tidy up the mess and to get my plans laid, so there was no difficulty in seeing him off. I feel that I have won the first game, when it was his service. Next time it will be my service, the score being one-love."*

forced by the 164th Division flown in from the Balkans–but without its vehicles; this was also the case with the parachute troops of the German Ramcke Brigade, and the Italian "Folgore" Division.

In the notes which he has left us, Rommel lays the blame for the failure of his last offensive on the way he was let down by the *Comando Supremo*, whose head, Marshal Cavallero, never stopped making him the most alluring promises. But it is difficult to accept this criticism, since it was no fault of Cavallero's that Malta was not neutralised and then besieged, instead of the boats of the British 10th Submarine Flotilla being once more able to use Malta's large harbour from the beginning of July. As a result, Italian supplies lost in transit, about six per cent in July, shot up to 25 per cent of equipment and 41 per cent of fuel in August; indeed, Cavallero's diary for the period reads like an obituary: "August 25. The *Pozarica* is torpedoed. August 27. The *Camperio* is set on fire. August 28. The *Dielpi* and the *Istria* are both sunk, the latter with all her crew. August 30. The *Sant'Andrea* is sunk with 1,300 tons of fuel for the D.A.K."

Another point is that Rommel's criticisms take no account of the fact that his supply lines had become far too long. To get from the front to Benghazi took a week, with a further five days to get to Tripoli for supplies. It is true that Tobruk was better placed, but it could only take small ships of up to 600 tons, and in any case had suffered very heavy attacks at the hands of the R.A.F. The responsibility for this state of affairs was Rommel's alone since, despite the doubts of Bastico, Cavallero, and Kesselring himself, he had insisted on exploiting his victories by going headlong after the enemy.

△ *One of Rommel's dual purpose 4-cm anti-aircraft guns. But as Montgomery had ordered his armour to fight purely defensively, as dug-in artillery, Rommel's highly effective 4- and 8.8-cm guns had to restrict themselves to A.A. fire.*

▽ *British infantry train for the day of the final offensive.*

The British Hawker Hurricane IID anti-tank fighter

Engine: one Rolls-Royce Merlin XX
12-cylinder V inline, 1,460 hp.
Armament: two 40-mm Rolls-Royce
B.F. or Vickers Type S cannon with 12
or 15 rounds per gun respectively, and
two .303-inch Browning machine guns.
Speed: 316 mph at 19,000 feet.
Ceiling: 33,500 feet.
Range: 480 miles.
Weight empty/loaded: 5,700/8,100 lbs
Span: 40 feet.
Length: 32 feet 2½ inches.
Height: 8 feet 9 inches.

The German plan

Rommel's plan of attack included some decoy movements by the Italian X and XXI Corps, reinforced by German elements. These would engage the enemy head-on and prevent him getting wind too soon of the plan of attack. These dummy attacks were to begin at 0200 hours, giving Rommel the whole night to take his armoured forces (consisting of the Italian XX Corps and the *Deutsches Afrika Korps*) through the left wing of the enemy's lines, and up to 30 miles past their starting point. After this he would regroup his armour and wheel to the north, with the intention of reaching the Alexandria road behind the 8th Army, which would thus be cut off from its communications, caught on the retreat, and annihilated. There would then be a threefold pursuit of the enemy:

1. the Bismarck group (the 21st Panzer Division and the 164th Division) would make for Alexandria;
2. the *Afrika Korps* (the 15th Panzer Division and the 90th Light Division) would cross the Nile at Cairo and immediately head for the Suez Canal; and
3. the Italian XX Corps (the "Ariete" and "Littorio" Armoured Divisions) and the "Trieste" Motorised Division would clean up any resistance in the Wadi Natrun area.

As Paul Carell has said, this plan had Rommel written all over it. And Colonel Bayerlein, chief-of-staff of the *Panzerarmee* at this time, has confirmed that it was a tried and tested Rommel tactic, which he had used at Tobruk, Gazala, and Marsa Matrûh. All very true–but the point was that it had been used so often that it was now worn out, and was too typical not to be seen through quite easily. In fact, both the Auchinleck/Dorman-Smith team and General Montgomery made their plans on the assumption that Rommel would do something like this: a deep eastward push into the southern sector of the El Alamein position, followed by a rapid straightening-up towards the Mediterranean.

When Montgomery assumed command (48 hours earlier than he was supposed to), the 8th Army was deployed as follows:

1. on the right, blocking the way to Alexandria, was Lieutenant-General William H. C. Ramsden's XXX Corps, made up of the 9th Australian, 1st South African,

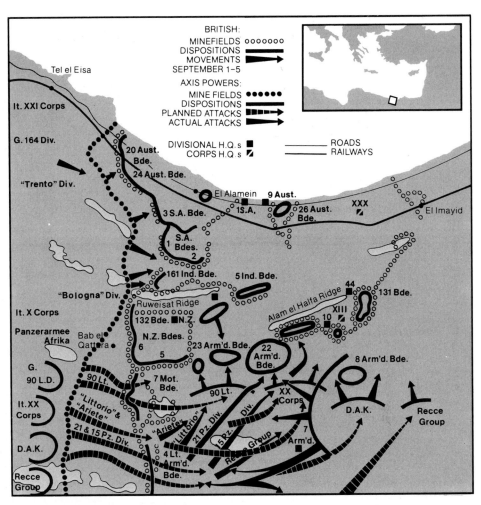

and 5th Indian Divisions; and

2. on the left, Lieutenant-General Brian Horrocks' XIII Corps had the New Zealand Division in the line with the 7th Armoured Division further south, for the purpose of slowing up Rommel's initial push and then making a flank attack as soon as he turned north.

These dispositions did not altogether please Montgomery; he thought in particular that Alam el Halfa ridge was too lightly defended, so he brought in the 44th Division, under Major-General I. T. P. Hughes, and also two armoured brigades of the 10th Armoured Division (a perfect example of the Montgomery "dynamism" mentioned earlier on). All in all, on August 31, the 8th Army had available 712 serviceable tanks, though this figure includes 164 Grants.

In spite of these reinforcements, Montgomery imposed an essentially defensive strategy upon his army. He thought that too often in the past the British tanks had been launched into attacks or counter-attacks that Rommel had cunningly channelled so as to bring them up against his redoubtable anti-tank guns. This battle would therefore be essentially an artillery duel, with tank movements restricted to

△ *The Battle of Alam el Halfa, Rommel's last attempt to push through to the Suez Canal. Montgomery had deployed his troops in masterly fashion, with the tanks at his disposal dug in as extra artillery. Rommel, his initial advance not being as fast as usual, found himself at dawn in a position where his forces could be defiladed by the heavy concentrations of artillery on the Alam el Halfa and Ruweisat Ridges. He therefore decided not to risk heavy casualties and pulled back. The last threat to Egypt was over.*
Overleaf: A Bristol Beaufighter I of the Western Desert Air Force. Ranging far behind the Axis lines, these aircraft, with their heavy offensive armament, were a constant thorn in the side of Rommel's already difficult supply problem.

△ *A British infantryman rushes forward for a local counter-attack. Such actions were fairly rare in this battle, however, dominated as it was by artillery and both sides' wish to avoid losses.*

exceptional cases; so his tanks dug in. "Don't let yourself get bitten!" he never tired of repeating to Horrocks, upon whose corps the brunt of the Axis offensive was soon to fall.

A British trap

An element of cunning was brought into the operation by Montgomery's chief-of-staff, Brigadier-General Francis de Guingand, who made up a false map showing the condition of the tracks, the positions of the areas of soft sand unusable by vehicles, and the minefield positions for XIII Corps' sector – all put in with more than a dash of fantasy. The next step was to fake in no-man's land an incident which would lead to the capture of this spurious document in such a way as not to arouse suspicion about its authenticity. This was brought about at the instigation of General Horrocks who, on being told that the precious map had disappeared from the wreck of the armoured car in which it had been left, telephoned Guingand thus: "Is that you Freddy? They've taken your egg away. Please God that they hatch out something from it." And, according to Colonel Fritz Bayerlein, they tended it with loving care until it did indeed hatch out on the night of August 30.

Rommel's lack of certainty

To launch his attack Rommel would have liked to take advantage of the full moon of August 26, but the supply difficulties mentioned above led to its postponement until August 30. That evening, just before H-hour, which had been fixed for 2200 hours, a stirring order of the day was read out to the troops, reminding them of their glorious past exploits, and exhorting them to the decisive effort:

"Our army, reinforced by new divisions, is moving in to annihilate the enemy.

"In the course of these decisive days, I expect every man to give of his best.

"Long live Fascist Italy! Long live Germany! Long live our glorious leaders!"

But Rommel was less certain of a successful outcome to the operation than his own proclamation indicated. Writing to his wife a few hours earlier, he had told her, after pointing out the deficiencies that still remained in his army:

"I've taken the risk, for it will be a long time before we get such favourable conditions of moonlight, relative strengths, etc., again. I, for my part, will do my utmost to contribute to success.

"As for my health, I'm feeling quite on top of my form. There are such big things at stake. If our blow succeeds, it might go some way towards deciding the whole course of the war. If it fails, at least I hope to give the enemy a pretty thorough beating. Neurath has seen the Führer, who sent me his best wishes. He is fully aware of my anxieties."

At 0200 hours on the 31st, the Italo-German motorised column reached the first British minefield. The D.A.K., consisting only of the 15th and 21st Panzer Divisions, was in the lead, followed by the Italian XX Corps, now commanded by General de Stefanis. Bringing up the rear was the 90th Light Division, which remained in close contact with the Italian X Corps, holding a pivotal position in the Axis line. All in all there were 515 tanks, of which 234 were German machines, including 26 of the new mark of Pzkw IV's mounting a 7.5-cm 43-calibre gun. The D.A.K. also had available 72 mobile 8.8-cm guns, but these were never used, as a result of the orders the astute Montgomery had given to his tanks to dig in as supplementary artillery.

The American M4A1 Sherman II medium tank

Weight: 30.2 tons.
Crew: 5.
Armament: one 75-mm M3 gun with 89 rounds, plus one .5-inch and two .3-inch Browning machine guns with 6,250 and 7,750 rounds respectively.
Armour: 75-mm maximum, 15-mm minimum.
Engine: one Continental 9-cylinder radial, 400 hp.
Speed: 25 mph.
Range: 115 miles.
Length: 19 feet 7 inches.
Width: 8 feet 9 inches.
Height: 9 feet 9 inches.

△ The mighty "88" was one of Rommel's most important weapons, but when he decided to pull back, even some of these were left behind, such as the one behind this British soldier curiously examining some of the detritus of the battle.

▷ Not only matériel was left behind. These are some of the 569 Germans and Italians listed as "missing" after the battle and who became prisoners of the 8th Army.

Axis withdrawal

By 0300 hours on the 31st, it had dawned on Rommel that things were not going with their usual smoothness. Fired on by the guns of the 7th Armoured Division, and bombed by the Desert Air Force, some German tanks were coming up against unmarked minefields, whilst others were getting bogged down on routes that had been marked as perfectly usable. So that instead of making a push of 30-odd miles into the enemy's lines, the Axis mechanised forces had only covered about ten. Rommel would consequently have to give up the wheel he had intended to make after an initial deep push; but if he turned north now, he would come under fire from the crest of Alam el Halfa ridge, where XIII Corps, with 64 artillery batteries, 300 anti-tank guns, and the same number of tanks, was waiting.

Shortly afterwards, even worse news reached Rommel: Major-General Georg von Bismarck, commanding the 21st Panzer Division, had been killed by a mine, and Lieutenant-General Walther Nehring, commanding the *Afrika Korps*, had been badly wounded in an air attack and replaced in the field by Colonel Bayerlein.

It was therefore no surprise that the D.A.K. attack on Hill 132, the highest point of the Alam el Halfa ridge, was repulsed; on its left, the Italian XX Corps fared no better—inevitably—in view of its light equipment; and the 90th Light Division, in the pivotal position, opposite the New Zealand Division, had its commander, Major-General Kleeman, seriously wounded in an air attack. The R.A.F., in fact, was everywhere, and on September 1 Rommel himself nearly met with the same fate as Nehring and Kleeman. Furthermore, despite the assurances showered on him by Cavallero and Kesselring, fuel supplies for the *Panzerarmee* were coming up more and more slowly. Accordingly, on the morning of September 3, Rommel took the decision to withdraw his troops.

First round to Montgomery

Preoccupied with his plans for a general offensive, Montgomery decided not to exploit this defensive success. It had cost the 8th Army 1,750 men and 67 tanks,

whilst Axis losses were 536 dead, 1,760 wounded, and 569 missing, together with 49 tanks, 55 guns, and 395 trucks captured or destroyed. These are the figures for the battle of Alam el Halfa, which General Mellenthin has described as follows:

"8th Army had every reason to be satisfied with this victory, which destroyed our last hope of reaching the Nile, and revealed a great improvement in British tactical methods. Montgomery's conduct of the battle can be assessed as a very able if cautious performance, in the best traditions of some of Wellington's victories."

The day after his victory, Montgomery wrote to a friend:

"My first encounter with Rommel was of great interest. Luckily I had time to tidy up the mess and to get my plans laid, so there was no difficulty in seeing him off. I feel that I have won the first game, when it was his service. Next time it will be my service, the score being one-love."

△ △ *A motor-drawn 40-mm Bofors anti-aircraft gun moves up towards the front.*
△ *One of Rommel's 536 dead, an Italian soldier.*

Hitler promises Rommel reinforcements

At about this time, Rommel, whose health was poor, went on sick leave. The Goebbels propaganda machine greeted him rapturously, and put all sorts of optimistic forecasts into his mouth; and on visiting Hitler he received the most alluring promises: the *Afrika Korps* would soon be strengthened by the 10th Panzer Division, and by the S.S. *Leibstandarte Adolf Hitler* Motorised Division, then stationed in France, and also by the 22nd Airborne Division which had just left the Crimea for Crete. He could also have a brigade of *Nebelwerfer* rocket-launchers, and 40 56-ton Pzkw VI Tiger tanks, which in firepower and protective armour far outclassed even the newest of Allied tanks. It is a sad fact, however, that by the fateful day of October 23, none of these reinforcements had reached him, whilst fresh troops and equipment were reaching the Allies at an ever-increasing rate.

Early September saw the arrival in Egyptian ports of the 300 Sherman tanks and 100 self-propelled 105-mm guns that a generous President Roosevelt had provided; of course, this equipment could not be used immediately as sand filters had to be fitted to the tanks, and the British crews had to be trained to get the best out of these American tanks which they had never seen before. Almost simultaneously, two new divisions fresh from Great Britain disembarked at Suez: the 51st Highland Division, soon to add El Alamein to its battle honours, and the 8th Armoured Division, which had only a short existence.

Middle East aerial forces were also being built up: four squadrons of two-engined North American B-25 Mitchell bombers, with a range of more than 1,200 miles, were delivered to Egyptian bases, and the Vickers Wellington bombers of Sir Arthur Tedder–and even the Fleet Air Arm's Fairey Albacores–underwent training to enable them to take part in the 8th Army's operations. The advantage in "flying artillery" thus passed over to the Allies, and played the same vital rôle in the offensive as it had done at the time of the Blitzkrieg.

These then, are the preliminaries of the Battle of El Alamein, which as we shall see in Chapter 75, was to complement Operation "Torch".